The Sexually Abused Child

SUE HERBERT 1996

THE
SEXUALLY
ABUSED
CHILD

*A Parent's Guide
to Coping & Understanding*

KATHLEEN FLYNN MACH, MSW

Family Insight Books
WILLIAMSBURG, MICHIGAN

Additional copies of this book may be ordered through bookstores
or by sending $9.95 plus $3.50 postage and handling to:
Publishers Distribution Service
6893 Sullivan Road
Grawn, MI 49637
(800) 507-2665

Publisher's Cataloging-in-Publication Data

Mach, Kathleen Flynn, 1954—
The sexually abused child: a parent's guide to coping
and understanding / Kathleen Flynn Mach—
Family Insight Books:
Williamsburg, Michigan.
p. ; cm.
Includes bibliographical references and index.
ISBN: 0-9640778-0-9
1. Sexually abused children. 2. Child molesting.
3. Abused children. I. Title.
HV6626.5.M33   1994
362.76—dc20   93-80905

Manufactured in the United States of America

10 9 8 7 6 5 4 3 2 1

Cover and text design by Heather Lee Shaw / PDS

For Dan and Andy

Contents

Preface

THE IDEA FOR THIS BOOK came several years ago from a young couple who suspected their daughter had been sexually abused. For months, they attributed her behavior changes to "the terrible twos," until she finally showed them with her doll what was happening to her. These parents felt angry, ashamed, and guilty for not seeing the signs sooner. They waited weeks before making an appointment with me, and spent that time feeling scared and worried. They had many questions, and were grateful for some answers. That's when I realized that a book about what to expect after a child has been abused could have given them some reassurance.

Reports of sexual abuse of children are on the rise, and statistics show that most children know the persons who abuse them.[1] While most parents take their job of providing support, love, and protection seriously, this doesn't always keep a child safe.

This book is designed to help parents and other caregivers cope when children have been abused. It suggests what can happen to families, and illustrates with specific cases. It was written for all parents and other concerned adults who are supportive and protective of children.

Some readers may be dealing with the painful aftermath of their child's sexual abuse. Others may have questions about abuse, or not know what to do if they suspect it. Some families may still be in shock about the identity of the abuser, especially if she is known to them.

Most of the information in this book is pertinent for every parent, but some issues, e.g., disbelieving your child, going to court, or caring about the abuser, affect only certain families. The reader is encouraged to take the information that "fits" for her family and situation.

This book isn't meant as a replacement for therapy or other types of support. It is meant as a first step to help parents and children begin the healing process after sexual abuse.

The case histories are composites drawn from cases I have seen in more than twelve years of practice as a clinical social worker. The cases are representative, but none is described exactly, for the sake of confidentiality.

Abuse of all kinds happens to both boys and girls, and in this book I have tried to alternate between the pronouns "he" and "she" for the sake of balance; in all cases where I use one, the other could as easily apply. This is also true for the word "parent." Parent can be interchanged with any caregiver or concerned person, such as a foster parent, legal guardian, or relative.

Sexual abuse can cause real problems, but it doesn't have to ruin a child's life. Healing can begin soon after the disclosure or discovery of sexual abuse if a child is shown compassion and concern, and given effective help. Supportive and loving parents or caregivers are often a child's greatest asset.

Acknowledgments

I AM GRATEFUL for the time and talents of the people who helped make this book a reality.

Special thanks go to Janis Burgess, J.D., Barbara Cross, M.S.W., Kathleen Coulborn Faller, Ph.D., Kathleen Gillissie, and Jan Proudfoot, M.S.W. who reviewed my manuscript and gave me invaluable suggestions and ideas.

Much appreciation is given to Sherry La Breck, my editor, Graydon De Camp, and Alex Moore, who coordinated the project.

Over the years, I have been touched by the trust and sharing of the many families I have seen in therapy. Some of their stories are told in this book, but only with identifying information changed to maintain confidentiality.

I have acknowledged all specific references to particular persons or books in the notes section, but if there are any omissions, it's a regrettable oversight. After years as a therapist, much of this information has become "second nature" to me, so some sources of information are either unknown or gathered from my experiences working with families.

This book is for all children and families who face the terrible ordeal of sexual abuse, but who fight back with courage, compassion, and strength. It is dedicated to my parents, Gert and Gene Flynn, and my husband and son, Dan and Andy Mach, who supported me with humor, patience, and love from the book's inception to its completion.

CHAPTER

1

Finding Out About the Abuse

Eleven-year-old Samantha waited two weeks before she told her mother that her babysitter was touching her "in wrong places." Samantha knew her mother had to work and knew there were few babysitters nearby. Samantha didn't want her mother to worry.

Cory, age three, began having terrible nightmares and started bed-wetting after he had already been toilet trained. He cried when his father gave him his bath, especially when he washed his penis. Cory's parents couldn't understand what was happening to their son until their nephew, who had spent the summer with them, was accused of molesting a neighbor boy.

Six-year-old Tina tearfully told her mother that her stepfather put his "pee-pee" between her legs and made her touch it. He had told Tina if she ever told, she would never see her mother again. Tina kept her frightening secret until a school program gave her the permission to tell.

Each child has a different way of telling about being sexually abused. Some children tell their parents or other caregivers directly; others are too little or too frightened to know the words to tell. Some children are prompted by television shows or school programs that talk about "good touch and bad touch." Some children never tell, and the abuse is not discovered. They can grow up with a terrible burden, and guilt and other emotional problems often interfere with their lives.

Child sexual abuse encompasses a wide spectrum of behavior. It can be any form of touching, exposing, or molesting a child's genitals, rectal area, breasts, or buttocks. It includes making a child touch or see an adult's genitals as a type of sexual arousal or having an adult watch children sexually touching one another. It refers to any sexual activity that gives the perpetrator gratification or financial benefit.[2] Child sexual abuse also includes lewd looks, sexual comments, denial of privacy, or ignoring boundaries or limits. Sexual abuse runs the gamut from just looking to intercourse.

The person who abuses the child, the perpetrator or sexual offender, fits no set model. The perpetrator can be the stereotypical "dirty old man," but more commonly is a family member, friend, or acquaintance. Perpetrators can be any age, race, or sex. They come from all income groups and walks of life.

Parents may have different reactions depending on who abused their child. It may be easier to cope if the perpetrator is an acquaintance or stranger, rather than a spouse or a best friend. Some adults may believe a child is being abused, but have questions or uncertainties, or are afraid to make a report for fear of being wrong. There are common elements no matter who abused the child, but as we'll see in later chapters, there are many reactions to all types of abuse and all kinds of abusers.

Some parents may suspect their child has been abused, but have no proof. Unfortunately, not all children can or will tell about being sexually abused. They may be too frightened or too young, or unable to understand the dynamics of the abusive relationship. Some children don't want to tell because they like the offender or don't want the attention, gifts, or "special" times to stop. Some children are threatened or feel too vulnerable.

A brother and sister, Greg, age four, and Heidi, age five, underwent terrible abuse including digital penetration, at the hands of their maternal great-uncle. Neither child dared to say a word because the uncle threatened that if they told, he would kill them, their mother, and their infant brother. This uncle emphasized his threat by killing one of their puppies from the new litter with his bare hands.

Warning Signs of Abuse

There are some warning signals for parents to look for if they suspect abuse. The following lists[3] outline signs parents may see in a sexually abused child:

Behavioral Signs:
- Nightmares or other sleep disturbances.
- Problems in school or with peers.
- Sudden changes in attitude or behavior, e.g., from open to secretive, or happy to depressed.
- Regressive behavior, e.g., returning to bed-wetting, thumbsucking, etc.
- "Pseudo" mature behavior, e.g., tries to act older than age (shown through dress, make-up, activities, etc.).
- Secrecy about a new "friend."
- Frequent unexplained absences from school.
- Fear of a certain person or vehement objection to being left with someone or somewhere.
- Truancy, running away, promiscuity, or prostitution (most common in adolescence).
- Self-mutilation or addiction to drugs, alcohol, or food (most common in adolescence).
- Drawings, writings, or school work of unusual or bizarre sexual themes.

- Excessive sexual curiosity or masturbation, especially with preschool age children. (Natural curiosity and masturbation are normal for children. It's a warning sign only when it happens a lot.)
- Unusual or explicit knowledge about sex (shown through language or behavior).
- Seductive behavior, sexual advances, or sex play towards peers or adults. (The child may be reenacting behavior exhibited towards him.)
- Suicide attempts.

Emotional Signs:
- Low self-esteem.
- Depression or withdrawal.
- Feeling hopeless or helpless.
- Lack of trust.
- Suicidal thoughts or intentions.

Physical Signs:
- Unexplained headaches, stomach aches, vomiting, fainting, blackouts, etc.
- Bed-wetting, soiling, or other related problems.
- Loss of weight or appetite, or weight gain.
- Problems such as itching, pain, or soreness in genital or anal areas.
- Unexplained injury of vagina, rectal opening, penis, or genital areas.
- Signs of physical abuse and neglect.
- Torn, stained, or bloody underclothes.
- Sexually transmitted disease, vaginal discharge, etc.
- Pregnancy in a child.

Family Signs:
- A child who avoids being home by leaving for school early, arriving late, etc.

- Unusual favoritism shown by one parent or caregiver to the point of treating one child differently than his siblings.
- Extreme hostility towards one parent or caregiver.
- A child who doesn't want to be left alone with one parent or caregiver.
- Inattentive, unconcerned, or overwhelmed parent(s) or caregiver(s).
- Jealous, overly protective, rigid, or controlling parent(s) or caregiver(s).
- Extreme jealousy by parent(s) of child or friends (especially boyfriends).
- Little or no respect for child's feelings or personal boundaries, e.g., excessive watching, spying, constant questioning, or sexually suggestive comments or actions.
- Few limits or boundaries in the family.
- Substance abuse in the family.

Usually, if sexual abuse is happening within the family, a child will show some reaction or response. If the abuser is the parent, children are especially vulnerable and lose the safety and protection every child should have in his home. Trust in the abusing parent is compromised, and most likely, completely gone. Some children may be reluctant to stay home and act afraid of the abuser. Others try to overcompensate, trying hard to please the abuser, thinking that the abuser's displeasure of him is the reason for the abuse (which it is not). Some children may seem distant, and try to avoid any involvement with the perpetrator (even appropriate family activities). Infants and young children may cry or avoid the perpetrator by running away or avoiding his gaze.

An abusing parent may be jealous, intrusive, or show the child little respect. He may avoid the child unless he is drunk, angry, or high. He may expect unrealistic or age inappropriate responses or reassurances from his child rather than another adult, e.g., seeking comfort or wisdom after a job loss or family tragedy.

Other times, nothing looks "wrong" in the relationship. Sometimes, conditions in the family, such as an emotionally absent parent (e.g., due to drug use or an overwhelming work schedule) may lead a child to feel alone and be more vulnerable to the advances of a perpetrator. Stressful family circumstances or role changes create conflict and sometimes change the family dynamics, leaving fewer or less structured boundaries.

The warning signs should only be used as a guide. Parents should not immediately suspect sexual abuse for every new change in their child. Much of this behavior (for example, bedwetting, school problems, or sleep disturbances) is seen in most children at some time. Other common factors, such as divorce, moving to another town, or having a new baby at home can prompt reactions. Certainly, each developmental stage in a child brings new concerns and behavior normal for that age. For instance, it's not unusual for a teenager to have more mood swings or to avoid being home, but it may be out of character for a younger child. Parents need to know their children, as well as what is expected behavior at a particular age.

Parents should be alert to the warning signs that are of a sexual nature, e.g., explicit knowledge about sex or having a sexually transmitted disease. Obviously, these types of signs are more probable signals that sexual abuse is happening than other behavior that is more common to children. Parents are urged to look at the whole picture of what is happening in their child's life. While sexual abuse is a cause for some behavior changes, it is certainly not the only cause. Sometimes, children may be reenacting sexual scenes they saw on television or in their parent's bedroom. Othertimes, children may be responding to other emotional stresses, such as a parent's alcoholism or neglect, or serious problems in school.

Some children feel it is their job to protect their parents, and they might hesitate to say much because they don't want to burden their parents with problems. Some children are particularly sensitive and may feel their concerns are minor compared to an illness, financial worries, or fighting within the family. One little girl, relieved that her often quarrelsome parents were finally getting along, did not want to "rock the boat" by telling them about a fondling incident. While such children might not tell their parents about their sexual abuse, they might tell someone else, such as a relative, school counselor, or friend, who in turn, tells the parents.

Parents can learn about their child's being sexually abused directly from their children or from someone else. On rare occasions, the perpetrator admits guilt first. Parents who suspect abuse may want to ask their child about it, thus giving them "permission" to talk about any abuse or fears. Parents of young children or non-verbal children may proceed with their belief that abuse has occurred because of behavior changes or other warning signals.

What to Do First

No matter how you find out about the abuse, the first thing to do is reassure your child that you love him and that the abuse was not his fault. Children do not seduce adults. If your child has told you directly, praise him for his honesty and his trust in you; assure him he did the right thing by telling. Whatever you do, believe your child. Children rarely make up such accusations, and when there have been accusations, there is usually an adult instigating the allegation. Let your child know he is not alone, that you will protect him, and that you will go through this together. While abuse is shocking and frightening, try not to act too shocked or frightened. Show your natural concern; your child knows you well enough to know when you are faking emotions. However, he is looking for and needing your calmness and support, and wants to know that you will help things be better for him.

If your child has told someone else about the abuse before telling you, the same support, belief, and protection is necessary.

Your child's reason for not telling you could have had something to do with his worry about your reaction. Your child should be assured that he's not responsible for you, but that you are responsible for him. If this undue protection is a child's pattern, it usually means there were already problems in the family. These issues need to be addressed, along with the feelings and reactions to sexual abuse. While your trust in your child may have been shaken, he needs to know you will be there for him now.

Be prepared to discuss the abuse at your child's request. While parents should not force children to talk about abuse, parents need to give the message that they are free and willing to discuss it anytime. As with all things, children take their cues from their parents and other trusted adults.

If children sense their parents are sincere that it's okay to talk, they usually will. Be careful not to send your child mixed messages, (e.g., telling him to come to you, but always being busy when he wants to talk), cutting him short when he talks about feelings, (e.g., "don't worry, it's not so bad"), or giving him body language cues that you really don't want to talk about the abuse, (e.g., always looking away or being distracted by the television). Never talking or trying not to think about the abuse will not make it go away. It happened, and the more reassuring a parent can be, the better it will be for the child.

Getting Medical Help

There are times when the need for a medical exam is obvious. If the sexual assault just happened, or if your child is bruised, bleeding, or in shock, seek medical care immediately. If your child has recurrent problems or complaints about his genital or rectal areas, make an appointment with a doctor. If you have any questions or doubts, it's better to seek care than to wonder and worry. Sometimes a child will complain of other physical problems as his way of "telling" about abuse.

Some medical findings can conclusively point to sexual involvement. For instance, if medical assistance is sought quickly enough after a rape, semen may be found that can be used as evidence. Sexually transmitted disease can also point to sexual abuse. If a five-year-old girl is found to have gonorrhea, odds are she's been abused.

Doctors have medical guidelines about what to look for in cases of sexual-abuse allegations. There is medical literature regarding what is normal and not normal for an anus, rectum, vagina, hymen, or the areas around these parts of the body. Medical findings may not be conclusive, but neither can they rule out sexual abuse. For example, redness around the vagina, yeast infections, a torn hymen, or rectal bleeding may have origins other than sexual abuse, but they can also be the result of sexual abuse. Unless there has been obvious damage from a severe trauma or repeated sexual manipulation of the genitals, most medical exams cannot conclude without a doubt the abuse happened.

However, building a court case should not be your prime reason for seeking medical care. If it gives you and your child peace of mind to get a check-up, then do it. However, be prepared for your child's being upset about the doctor's touching his "privates." Assure your child that you will be there with him and that it's okay for a doctor to check him to see if there are any problems.

Steps to Take

While you are not ashamed of your child, neither should you make the abuse part of the public grapevine. Key people do need to know what happened —the police, child-protection worker, and other support people— but a distant relative you hear from only once a year doesn't have to know, nor do your child's classmates. Even if you feel certain people should know (e.g., your child's school grades have fallen dramatically and you want the teacher to know what happened), choose what you say carefully. Every detail need not be disclosed. You can control how you will respond to your child; you cannot control others' responses or prejudices.

By the same reasoning, be careful where you seek support for yourself and your child. Some "help" can be more damaging than reassuring. While you can't always predict another person's reaction, you can make an educated guess about the people you know. Avoid asking for support from people who tend to be judgmental, who frequently discount children's feelings, or who believe "the adult" is always right. Seek spiritual guidance if it comforts you, but you should know that some spiritual advisors may stress forgiveness of the perpetrator. Forgiveness may come later, but it's not essential for healing. Ask about support groups and competent counselors and therapists. Read books about abuse. Find out information from the child-protection worker or law enforcement officer involved with your family. Remember, there are still many people who don't understand the dynamics of sexual abuse, who think abuse is "no big deal" and a child should just forget it and carry on, or who tend to blame the child. You don't need these people now; they will not be helpful to you.

Although your child has been hurt, it is best to keep things as normal as you can. Don't become an overindulgent parent by breaking the rules so your child gets anything he wants. What he probably wants is that the abuse never happened, but unfortunately you cannot give him that. Your child doesn't need to feel any different from how he might already feel; he needs the stability and consistency of his home and family. You need to support the positive steps your child takes, praise his strengths, and encourage him to carry on with his life.

Of course, you should make some allowances for your child's behavior and be more sensitive to his emotional needs. Expect some moodiness, tearfulness, or regression. Your child might go back to bed-wetting when toilet training was already completed;

an outgoing child might become shy; you might see an increase in nightmares. As we'll see in a later chapter, each child reacts differently.

While there is no guarantee that there will be swift and appropriate justice, your child needs to know that you will back him up. In the initial stage of finding out about the abuse, you may not know what is going to happen. Be honest with your child; let him know as much as you can, but don't give any false assurances. He may have to repeat his story several times. He may have to go to court, which can be long, drawn-out, and scary. He may have to talk with a counselor or therapist or get a medical exam. Don't jump the gun with a lot of "what ifs," but be prepared.

It's important to know that just because the abuse has stopped, everything is not over. In some cases, it may seem as if things are just beginning. Remember that the healing process is just that — a process. While your child may never forget what happened, abuse does not have to change the course of his life. As you will see in later chapters, there are many ways of dealing with sexual abuse.

2

Reporting the Abuse

Each state has agencies that investigate the physical and sexual abuse of children. Often, a child-protection agency investigates when the alleged perpetrator is someone responsible for the child's health and welfare, such as a parent or other adult household member. Law enforcement agencies (police or sheriff's department) usually investigate complaints against those persons not directly responsible for the child, such as neighbors or strangers. Frequently, child-protection and law enforcement agencies work together.

Certain professions, including doctors, social workers, and teachers, are obligated by law to report any reasonable suspicion of child abuse. However, anyone can make an anonymous report if that person has suspicions or concerns. Sometimes, this anonymity has led to concerned, but misinformed calls, and other times, to vengeful callers' making untrue accusations.

Many parents initiate the report when their children first tell them about being abused or when they have cause to suspect abuse. However, some parents may hesitate to report the alleged abuse if the perpetrator is known to the family, if the abuse seems to be minor, or if they want to protect their children from the onslaught of the "system." No matter how well-intentioned parents might be, it's advisable to check with the authorities. While your call may not lead to any official action, it may give you peace of mind. However, parents who knowingly protect an offender over their children could be considered negligent and face the possibility of criminal charges. Sexual offenders are usually involved in more than one offense. Even if your child is safe now because of your knowledge and protection, other innocent children are at risk.

While almost all reports of alleged abuse are checked, some cases don't warrant any intervention and are screened out. For example, two fifteen-year-old boys flirting with a well-developed but frightened twelve-year-old girl is not sexual abuse. The girl might need support and guidance to handle future situations, and the boys should get a lesson in appropriate behavior, but it's not a child-protection case. On the other hand, any report involving fondling, rape, exploitation, etc. should be investigated. If there is a belief that a child is in imminent danger, the investigation should be started within 24 hours. All other investigations are usually started within 72 hours. Usually, within a month, a decision must be made by the child-protection team whether there is enough credible information to warrant an ongoing child-protection case. If not, the case is closed or denied. If there are continuing concerns, the case is kept open, with the possibility of court involvement.

When the Investigation Begins

Once an investigation begins, your child could be interviewed by a law enforcement officer, a child-protection worker, or by both. Depending on the age of the child and other circumstances, including the identity of the alleged perpetrator, a child could be interviewed with or without the parents present. Sometimes, there is a concern that parents unknowingly influence their children and their responses, even if the parents don't say anything during the interview. Some children will be more open with a stranger; others are reluctant to tell anyone other than a family member about the abuse. One little boy readily told a male detective about his abuse, but said nothing to a female investigator. He was embarrassed saying the word "penis" to a "strange lady." Usually, very young children are interviewed with their parents. Normally, these children feel safer with their parents present, and frequently the parents help interpret the language of pre-schoolers. However, if a parent is suspected of abuse, other arrangements can be made. In one case, a little girl was interviewed by the child-protection worker at her nursery school with her teacher there for support.

Where a child is interviewed depends on such factors as time, convenience, and availability of the persons involved. Care should be taken by the investigator to create an environment where a child feels comfortable. The back of a police car or the place where the alleged abuse happened would certainly not be the best places for an interview. Often, an investigator sees older children at school in a private setting, such as the counselor's office. If children are interviewed without their parents' knowledge, the parents should be notified afterwards.

Children may have questions about the interview process. Parents and investigators should reassure them with honest answers. It's better to say, "I don't know," than to give children the answers they may want to hear, but may later turn out to be untrue. Some children may want to know what will happen to them next. They may ask what will happen to the perpetrator and whether they'll be safe. They may want to know if their friends or teachers have to know about the abuse or whether the information will be on the television or in the newspaper. If they are audio or videotaped, they may ask who will hear or see the tape. They may want to know if they're in trouble for telling. The list is endless. As a parent, you may anticipate some of your child's questions. However, children think of questions and worry about things that no adult may even think about. Ask your child if there are any worries, concerns, or fears.

Professionals who interview children regarding sexual abuse allegations usually have received a great deal of training. Ideally, they are careful to be objective, observant, and considerate of the child. They try to make the child feel at ease, and often may ask non-threatening questions about school, friends, or interests before talking about the alleged abuse. They realize that some children can be easily influenced and they are careful not to ask leading questions or "put words in a child's mouth." The interviewers usually ask open questions such as "what happened?," rather than more direct questions that could only be answered by yes or no. Once the child reveals more information, that information can be used in other questions.

> Natalie, age nine, told her school counselor, that her nineteen-year-old cousin, Ted, had been fondling her and hinting at "going all the way." The counselor reported it to the Child Protection Agency, and a child-protection worker interviewed Natalie at school with her mother's prior knowledge. The following are highlights of the interview:
>
> CPW: The counselor told me about your cousin, Ted. Can you tell me about Ted?
>
> Natalie: I hate him. He touched me.
>
> CPW: He touched you... Where did Ted touch you?
>
> Natalie: In my privates (pointing to her genital area).
>
> CPW: What did Ted do?
>
> Natalie: He pulled down my underpants and put his hand right on my privates. He grabbed me and it hurt. He made jokes about getting ready for when I'm a woman. I hate him...
>
> CPW: How many times did this happen?
>
> Natalie: A lot.
>
> CPW: Do you remember the last time?
>
> Natalie: It was Sunday. My Mom and Aunt Rita went out to dinner and Ted was supposed to watch me and my brother...

Obviously, not all children will be this forthcoming with information, but often they are. Sometimes, interviewers use anatomically correct dolls (dolls with accurate body parts, including anal openings, genitals, and breasts) if the child is having difficulty using words to show what happened. Other times, anatomical pictures or drawings may be used to help with the interview.

When children are too young or unable to speak for themselves, the investigators may rely on information from parents or caregivers, a doctor's report or physical exam, or an evaluation by a therapist or counselor. Of course, the investigation also involves talking with the alleged perpetrator, but this should be done without the child present.

Sometimes, the entire investigation can last months. In the case of very young children, there may be a waiting period until the child is able to talk about the sexual abuse. Often, toddlers or preschoolers are aware of what happened, but lack the words to express themselves.

Some parents worry that once sexual abuse is reported, their families will enter the unknown world of the "system," and not be able to get out, even if they want to. We've all seen news reports of official bungling and injustice. Such cases are rare, however, and as we'll see in a later chapter, there are safeguards to prevent this from happening.

3

Your Child's Reaction to the Abuse

Just as children have different shapes, sizes, and personalities, their coping styles may differ. The way a particular child handles being abused will depend on many factors, including her own strengths, age, support systems, frequency of the abuse, extent of the abuse, and who abused her.

One of the worst scenarios is a child who is raped by a threatening, violent person who lives in the home. Other adults in the family might not be much help because they, too, are afraid of the violent person. On the other hand, a one-time fondling incident by a family acquaintance where the child told her parents immediately and they supported and protected her, may cause few, if any, problems.

Children have different limitations and strengths. Some are "survivors" and do well even under the most horrible circumstances. Others have a low tolerance for stress and seem more frail. Most fall somewhere in the middle. It is important to know your child's strengths. However, be careful not to underestimate or overestimate her. No one really knows how they would react until it happens. For instance, just because your child seemed inconsolable after her grandfather died, it doesn't meant she'll "fall apart" because of abuse. On the other hand, just because your child has always seemed mature, it doesn't mean she can handle the aftermath of the abuse alone.

Your child's age is an important factor in determining her reaction. The difference between a three-year-old's understanding of what happened and a ten-year-old's is great. An older child may bring with her all types of emotional baggage —guilt, the "dirtiness" of the situation, or mistrust. A younger child may know something is not right, but not understand the emotional dynamics of the abuse.

Your support is essential for helping your child. The people a child loves the most —usually parents, grandparents, or other family members— make a big difference in how the child views the abuse and herself. The key people are the primary caregivers. If the child feels loved, supported, and safe, the outcome is usually good. If the key people do not believe the child, then she'll feel betrayed a second time and begin to think she did something wrong. It can be confusing (and sometimes devastating) to a child if parents are divided on their feelings about abuse.

> Marta always seemed to be "Daddy's little girl," and the two
> of them were inseparable. When Marta's paternal
> stepgrandfather molested her, her father did not believe her.
> Her mother did. The family took sides and Marta felt in the
> middle. She became distant and blamed herself for all the
> problems in the family.

Even if parents are supportive of their child, the child may misinterpret the parents' behavior or feelings. A child who has been abused is especially sensitive to emotions and reactions. While you don't have to constantly explain yourself to your child, it could lessen problems if you shared some of your feelings. For instance, if your child sees you crying, let her know you feel sad that something hurtful happened to her, but that you're fine and will be there for her. If your child sees you crying after a fight with your spouse or companion, let her know that you are having a disagreement, and you will take care of it; it has nothing to do with her. If you are acting differently toward your child, try to catch yourself before you do it. Better yet, discuss your concerns with someone: a therapist, understanding friend, or a support group.

The long-term effects on a child are usually going to be different if the abuse happened once than if it happened weekly over a period of years, or involved kidnapping, violence, or rape. Many children suffer no long-term effects. It depends on the type of abuse and the amount of support and help they receive. There is no way to know how devastating or frightening abuse was for someone else. Only the victim knows. Yet, most of the time, the healing process is quicker if the abuse occurred once or infrequently. However, this is only a guideline. Don't dismiss anyone's reactions to abuse. Even one abusive incident can create distrust, fear, questioning, and self-doubt. This is particularly true if the perpetrator is someone close to the child. Even when there is no overt abuse, a child is still affected. Lewd looks, sexual comments, and lack of appropriate boundaries create an uncomfortable and abusive environment.

The relationship of the perpetrator to your child is very important. The impact for your child tends to be much greater if the perpetrator is someone well-known to the family rather than a stranger or acquaintance. It becomes even more devastating if the perpetrator is someone the child loves. An exception to this could be the stranger rape or molestation where the child might have been beaten, kidnapped, threatened, or left near death.

Children Abusing Children

It is important to note that children do sexually abuse other children. It's also important to recognize that there is a vast difference between two four-year-old children exploring their bodies and playing "doctor" and a fifteen-year-old babysitter sticking a finger up a five-year-old's vagina. In order to define abuse among children, several things must be taken into account: age, power or force, and maturity and understanding. If there is a big age difference, it's abuse; if one child overpowers another with physical strength and power or uses force or threats, it's abuse; and if one child understands what's going on and the other doesn't, it's abuse.

> Todd, age fourteen, was known as the neighborhood show-off. On a dare, Todd pretended to like Emma, a neighbor girl who was one year older than Todd but functioned intellectually as a six-year-old. On the pretext of taking her for ice cream, Todd took Emma to a secluded spot and fondled her breasts and genitals.

Just as sexual abuse happens between adult family members and children, it also happens between brothers and sisters. Sibling sexual abuse is not uncommon. Usually, the dynamics between the perpetrator and the victim are similar to adult-child abuse. Often, fear, betrayal, and shame are common reactions. The abused child has lost the sanctity of her home, and frequently is threatened "not to tell."

In recent years, there have been more reports of children abusing other children. These youthful perpetrators must take responsibility for their actions, but they also need compassion and help. Fortunately, treatment programs and therapy groups are becoming more available for these young offenders.

Most children who abuse other children come from troubled families and many were themselves physically and sexually abused. Many received no help for their problems. However, some children are reacting to the increased exposure to sexually suggestive or explicit information. One twelve-year-old girl with no reported family problems or history of being sexually abused was accused of molesting a child she was babysitting. She stated she had seen these acts on a cable television movie and thought she would try them out.

How Children React to Abuse

There are no formulas for knowing how your child will react when sexually abused. It is impossible to say that if certain factors are present, your child will react a particular way. For each abused child, there is a unique reaction. However, there are some common patterns. You may have seen some of these reactions before the abuse was disclosed or discovered. You may see some of them after the abuse is reported. Obviously, every change in a child is not a response to abuse. However, if you know your child has been abused, expect some behavior change. Your child may experience one or several of these reactions, or something completely different.

The following are some reactions you might see in your child:
• Bed-wetting.
• Nightmares or sleeplessness.
• Physical complaints or problems.
• Needing to know where parent(s) are at all times (clinging).
• Fear of dark or other unexplained fears.
• Fear of strangers or new situations.
• Wanting to sleep with parent(s).
• Masturbation.
• Exploring, touching, or acting out sexually with siblings or peers.
• Anger, yelling, kicking, or breaking things.
• Ignoring or disobeying parent(s) or other authority figures.
• Intense worry (about parent(s), self, going to court, or the perpetrator's coming back).
• Depression or grief.
• Not wanting to talk about the abuse or constantly wanting to talk about the abuse.
• Sullen or moody behavior.
• Distrust of others.
• Feelings of guilt or humiliation.

- Feeling dirty or somehow changed.
- Emotional numbness or avoidance of feelings.
- Truancy or running away.
- Development of psychological problems.
- Seductive or promiscuous behavior.*
- Drug or alcohol abuse.*
- Attempted suicide.*

The list is not meant to scare you, but show you the wide range of reactions. Some reactions are expected, especially under certain circumstances. Feelings are normal and important. It's the actions a person takes as a result of the feelings that can be harmful.

It is understandable for a child who has been molested by a stranger to be fearful of new people. It makes sense that most children have some anger or distrust about what happened to them. Your child needs ways to feel safe. If she wants a night light on, or wants you to be nearby (especially right after the abuse), respect her wishes. This is not to say you must change your life around to accommodate your child, but listen to her needs. Remember how you feel when you are scared or nervous or worried; you probably want a friendly face, a hug, and some reassurance.

No one knows exactly how they're supposed to act, but be responsive to your child's needs. Almost always, a child will show some type of reaction. If your child shows anger, that's okay. But it may not be okay that she breaks a window. There need to be limits. If your child wants to talk nonstop about what happened, let her, but also tell her that others have the right to talk at the dinner table, too. If your child spends her free time in her bedroom "doing nothing," it's fine, as long as you check on her

* Usually happens in adolescence, often after repeated or brutal abuse.

periodically and let her know you're there if she wants you.

There are some reactions that are not "okay." These responses usually happen after a child has been abused for a long time. Often, these reactions —promiscuity, drug or alcohol abuse, and attempted suicide— begin while the abuse is still going on. Too often, they seem to the child to be the only escape from the abuse and the feelings of worthlessness, guilt, and anger.

> Kerrie's earliest memories were of a drunken father and the
> fighting and yelling in her home. She recalled a Christmas
> morning spent crying after her father gave her mother a
> black eye. Kerrie's father only spoke quietly and kindly to her
> when he came into her room night after night to touch her.
> The older she got, the more he expected from her. Kerrie
> didn't dare tell anyone at first. After a while she felt no one
> would help because she was guilty, too. When Kerrie's father
> started wanting intercourse, Kerrie ran away from home,
> and became involved with drugs and prostitution.

There are times when the only "escape" for a sexually abused child is to deny, avoid, or "forget" the experience. In situations of brutal and ongoing abuse, some children develop psychological disorders as a means of coping. Some adults who were abused as children report they experienced out-of-body or dissociative reactions or developed multiple personalities. They removed themselves mentally as a way of avoiding both the actual abuse and the feelings associated with it. Their lives got divided into compartments, so that the abuse might affect only one "part" of their lives. For instance, if the first personality was the one that got abused, the second personality could be the one that excelled in school or idolized the abuser. Some children remember only parts of the sexual abuse or the situations surrounding the abuse, but not the abusive acts.

While these are drastic aberrations and cause the child serious problems, it shows the strength of the abused child who wants to survive. These reactions are real. They are the mind's way of surviving terror, betrayal, and harm. By most accounts, these reactions occur after ongoing, brutal, or life-threatening abuse. Usually, such reactions occur when the perpetrator is well-known to the child, but sometimes they're a reaction to the terror of stranger rape or molestation. Most children do not develop these reactions, but it's important to realize these things do happen. Most of the children who develop serious psychological problems do not have someone to believe them, support them, look for warning signs of abuse, or protect them.

Time Factors

A timetable is impossible, but be concerned if the reactions increase, or fail to lessen over several months. An older child will probably never forget what happened to her, and it may influence her life, but it is unhealthy to let it cloud her entire outlook on her life and goals. However, do expect some regression if you go to court, talk with a therapist, or see the perpetrator. Anything that clearly reminds your child about the abuse may prompt some new or regressive behavior.

> Gary, age ten, reacted to his molestation with worry, guilt, and distrust. With the help of his foster parents and group therapy, he did extremely well. However, when the court procedures started six months later, Gary began to have restless nights and seemed to cry constantly. When his new fears were addressed at home and in therapy, he was able to testify in court and the perpetrator was found guilty.

Sometimes, a child seems to cope extremely well in the early stages after the abuse has been discovered, but may have difficulty later on. There could be many reasons for this. She may feel safe and protected initially, but when things get back to normal she feels lost; she may have thought that once the sexual abuse was over, things would be fine, but she didn't expect the reminders of ongoing court procedures, or the delayed reactions to stress and worry. She may have tried to put on a good front at first, but she kept thinking about the abuse and blamed herself or felt differently. She may not have known how the knowledge of the abuse would change her family.

Appropriate Pleasures

Many parents are shocked when their children seem disappointed after the sexual abuse ends. Quite frankly, some sexual involvement can be pleasurable and to a child who knows nothing about adult boundaries, or who longs for attention, stroking or touching of her breasts and genitals or other types of sexual involvement can be soothing, calming, or just feel good.

> Tanya's day care provider would sit with Tanya on her lap
> touching her vagina with slow strokes and call it their "quiet
> time." Tanya enjoyed the touching and began to expect it.
> Their "quiet time" increased, and Tanya would resent it
> when other children were there and no touching happened.
> To compensate, Tanya began masturbating at home.

For some children, no matter how old they are, the sexual involvement is the only time they may see a more "gentle" side of the perpetrator. Other children feel special or excited by the attention of the perpetrator. Mixed emotions of anger, guilt, and excitement may be present.

Sally was old enough to know that what her Youth Group Leader was doing was wrong. She felt tremendous guilt and blamed herself. Yet, she was thrilled by the attention and the secret meetings, feeling more like a princess than an ugly duckling.

If your child feels at a loss after the abuse has stopped, other, more acceptable ways of feeling good need to be established. Your child should know that what the perpetrator did was wrong, but that she was not bad for feeling pleasure. It is wrong for an adult to rub a child's vagina for self-pleasure; it is acceptable to give her a hug or a back rub. Abuse is when someone sexually abuses a child for pleasure and power. The child's pleasure is secondary or (more likely) not even considered. Naturally, all loving parents get pleasure from giving their children a hug or a similar show of affection, but their motives are not sexual or seductive. They are comforting and loving.

Even an "innocent" show of affection is not appropriate if a child doesn't want it. Never force your child to hug or kiss someone she does not want to. While being made to kiss Great Aunt Thelma is not abuse, it doesn't allow your child the freedom and respect to choose physical touching. Children who have been abused may be particularly sensitive to unwanted touching, no matter how innocent.

You may need to explore with your child appropriate and healthy forms of physical self-pleasure. The range may vary from family to family, depending on values and personal or religious beliefs. Any form of pleasure needs to be harmless and agreed upon. There should never by any force or coercion. Even "gentle persuasion" is wrong. Physical pleasures can include hugging, kissing, cuddling, back rubs, or stroking hair. While you may not encourage masturbation, a child touching herself (in privacy) is neither wrong nor unusual (given certain limits). Your child needs to know that the sexual abuse, whether it was fondling or intercourse, was not acceptable. A young child may have difficulty understanding that it's okay to get undressed for a physical exam or a bath, but not for the sexual touching. You should be patient and let your child know the differences and reasons.

When Your Child Cares About the Perpetrator

It can be confusing for both the parents and the child if the child still has loving feelings toward the perpetrator. Many parents cannot understand how their child can still love someone who hurt them. Even some children who were brutally abused still express love toward the perpetrator. In almost all instances, the perpetrator is well-known to the child, whether she lived with the child or knew the child from another setting. There is a relationship beyond the abuse.

> Frankie was removed from his home after his mother abused
> him. While his extended family rallied around him, Frankie
> thought they would get angry if he said he missed his mother.
> He was angry about the abuse and didn't feel safe around his
> mother, but he also remembered the times they planted the
> garden or laughed over a television show.

It is important to let your child know it's okay to still care about the perpetrator. Don't make your child feel guilty about feelings because feelings and emotions can't be turned on and off. However, your child needs to know that what the perpetrator did was wrong and why it was wrong. Explain that she can care about someone or love them and still be angry about what happened. You can talk with your child about the good times (if any) with the perpetrator, and let her grieve that things will never be the same after the disclosure of the sexual abuse. Depending on the situation, court involvement, and the relationship of the child to the perpetrator, there may be supervised visitation or eventually, after treatment or jail, reconciliation. In many instances, the child never sees the offender again. Whatever the outcome, let your child talk about the perpetrator. Most children can understand that they can have loving feelings, but still dislike what happened to them. If there continues to be much confusion or excessive talk or concern about the perpetrator, discuss your concerns with someone you trust. As a parent, you may have mixed emotions about your child's feelings about the perpetrator. You need to work through that emotionally, and discuss it.

Most parents can cope with and understand behavior or mood changes in their child for a limited period. However, some things are too frightening to handle alone, and sometimes a child seems to get worse, not better. The best advice is to get some help and ask questions as soon as you find out about the abuse. Talk with someone who is experienced in working with sexual-abuse victims and their families. The child-protection worker and law enforcement officer can give you help and suggestions. A visit to a therapist or counselor could prove invaluable. While there are no quick fixes, getting professional help will give you some answers and guidance.

CHAPTER

4

Parents' Feelings and Reactions

Just as each child responds differently, each parent has his own reaction to his child's being abused. Feelings can range from numbness to rage. Many parents want revenge; others want to forget it, pretending the abuse never happened. Most reactions are tied to the factors discussed in the previous chapter —your child's age, frequency of the abuse, extent of the abuse, and who did it.

No matter what your personal feelings, your child needs you to be calm, supportive, and understanding. This is not to say it's wrong to show any emotions, but your child must feel you are in control and will take care of him, rather than thinking he must hide his feelings. Above all, trust and believe your child.

The need to be calm can take its toll on many parents. Many couples become angry with each other, perhaps for not doing enough or blame each other rather than being supportive. Some single parents are angry at the absent parent or blame themselves for not being Super Mom or Super Dad. Some parents have never been through such a traumatic experience. For others, a child's abuse triggers old feelings or unexplained reactions.

Dave, a likable, easy-going man, had been divorced for several years, but he remained friends with his ex-wife, and they usually agreed on their son's upbringing. When his son was molested, Dave became angry and moody. Not only did he worry about his son, but he was angry with his ex-wife for allowing their son to walk to the store where the abuse had happened. Dave knew his anger was irrational and focused on the wrong person; he should have been angry with the perpetrator, but he wasn't. Somehow he felt his ex-wife had betrayed their son. After some thought, he realized he was angry with himself for feeling he was not there to protect his son.

Many parents feel tremendous guilt. They think if they had been more alert, more protective, or more open with their child about life's dangers, the abuse might not have happened. Perhaps that is true, probably it is not. Unfortunately, even well-informed and protected children do get abused. While children must have the tools and knowledge to protect themselves and suspect potential danger, all it takes is one time of being overpowered, frightened, or threatened by a perpetrator. Whatever guilt parents may feel should be overshadowed by the fact that they did not commit the abuse, someone else did.

Most parents do all they can to provide a safe environment for their children. The perpetrator is responsible for the abuse, not the parent. It's true that some parents are too lax with rules or don't screen potential harm for their children. Some parents are alcoholics or drug abusers who might put their own highs ahead of their child's safety. Other parents know the abuse is going on or suspect it, but don't say anything for fear of the perpetrator or the consequences. There are parents who are too emotionally tied to the perpetrator and the child becomes the sacrifice. Some parents have few boundaries or limits on acceptable behavior. It does happen, and these parents need both help and consequences for their abusive actions. Their children need to be in safe, protective, and loving environments. Fortunately, most parents are conscientious, loving, and concerned.

You cannot be with your child every minute of the day, especially a school age child. You cannot get a police report or psychological test on every person with whom your child comes into contact. You have to trust some people sometimes. Unfortunately, there are those who betray that trust, and those who enter your child's life to do harm.

The urge to kill, maim, and get revenge are all common responses when your child has been abused. Clearly, it would be wrong to do any of those things. Most parents respond powerfully when their child has been hurt, especially when the harm was intentional. If you react with aggression, your child may feel guilty for upsetting you and feel confused because the person he counted on for control has lost it.

Do what you need to do to release some of the anger safely — jog, punch a punching bag, scream, write a journal, talk, join a support group, get therapy— but don't lose sight of who was the victim.

Your child is looking toward you for guidance. Your anger will not go away in a day or a week. In fact, you will probably always feel angry about what happened to your child. What is important is what you do with your anger and how you express it. Don't let this ruin your life or trust in others.

Many parents are saddened and grieve for the lost innocence of their child. The fairy tale view of childhood is gone once your child has been violated. The unfairness and sometimes fearsomeness of the real world has been thrust upon your child. While your child will probably heal, he may never be completely trusting again. There needs to be some normal caution about the world; unfortunately, your child got this painful lesson the hard way.

When the Parent Was Abused

One of the most difficult situations for parents is when they were sexually abused as children. The amount of guilt, anger, and sadness may be even more for these parents than for parents who were not abused. Even if a parent thought he had successfully dealt with his own feelings about the abuse, his child's abuse may reawaken painful old emotions. If a parent never made peace with himself about the abuse, or never even talked about it, the knowledge that his child has been abused could be devastating.

Those parents who kept the secret of their abuse may feel that their silence caused their child's abuse. On the contrary, most of these parents were vigilant in protecting their children and vowed their children would never be abused. For them, the knowledge of their child's abuse is a shock and a tragedy. For some, it is hard to believe their children were abused because self-protection was drilled into them at a young age. What some of these parents don't understand is that for many of the very same reasons they kept silent, their children kept silent.

> Both Jack and his son were the oldest in their family. Both took on adult responsibilities as children. Both were abused as young boys. Although Jack thought he raised his son to be open about problems, he could not understand why his son didn't come to him first about the abuse. Just like Jack, his son thought it would be better to suffer the consequences of the abuse than to upset the family.

Children keep abuse secret for many reasons —shame, fear, guilt, or feeling that no one will believe them. In previous generations, abuse was rarely discussed and frequently dismissed. Some children did tell, only to be punished, ridiculed, or disbelieved. Most children showed some signs or behavior changes, only to be misunderstood.

Some adults who were abused as children do not consciously remember it, but know that something has always felt odd in their lives. They do not remember the origin of their feelings of distrust, fear, or powerlessness. Some completely deny the experience because it was too awful to remember. Some adult survivors of sexual abuse are jolted into remembering it by experiences with their own children.

Each person has his own story about his abuse. Each person has his own reason for telling or not telling, remembering or not remembering. There are many powerful accounts from men and women who were abused as children whose experiences parallel the experiences of most abused children from previous generations (see Appendix C —For Parents and Caregivers Who Were Abused As Children). If you were abused as a child and are having problems dealing with your child's abuse, it's not too late to talk about your own history and how it affected you. It may not be too late to confront the perpetrator or protect your children from the perpetrator, if he is known to you. Remember, you did not cause your own abuse, and your history did not cause your child's abuse. Just because you were abused, and your child has been abused, doesn't mean you subconsciously planned it or did something to set your child up for abuse. You did not ask to be abused, or for your child to be abused. Most parents do all they can to protect their children: giving them cues to make them cautious, discussing people and situations to avoid, giving them permission to say "no," and avoiding secrets.

There are support and therapy groups for adults who were sexually abused as children. In order to help yourself and your child, find out where such a group meets. If you are uncomfortable with a group situation, get some individual or family therapy, or at least consult a therapist about your own past, fears, and worries.

Unfortunately, there are families in which incest and sexual abuse are a tradition. The family secret may not be much of a secret, but everyone tries to keep it – often to protect family members and sometimes the perpetrator. Some families believe it's normal for a little sexual experimentation between adults and children. Any sexual involvement between adults and children is wrong.

Jeanna was the oldest of three sisters and two brothers. When her grandfather first molested her, he told her he would spare the younger siblings if she didn't tell anyone. Her grandfather used the same story on each of the children. No one ever told because they thought they were protecting the others. When Jeanna had children of her own, she tried to keep them from being alone with her grandfather. It wasn't until Jeanna's daughter was propositioned by her grandfather that the story began to unfold and the family secret was revealed.

When the Abuser Is Someone You Thought You Could Trust

Equally troubling for a parent is when the abuse was perpetrated by someone well-known and trusted by the family. If the abuse is caused by a spouse or lover, it means a double loss. There can be a wide range of reactions including anger, disbelief, betrayal, and guilt. Many parents question their judgment, especially if the perpetrator lives with the family.

> Madeline and Barry dated each other for nearly a year before they began living together. Madeline's children, including a thirteen-year-old daughter, Kara, lived with them. Madeline worked afternoons, while Barry worked during the day, leaving him home at night with the children. When Barry started to walk around the house naked, Kara told her mother. Barry claimed Kara just caught him running from the shower to the bedroom. When Barry started inviting Kara into the bathroom while he showered, Kara refused, but told her mother. Barry explained he had run out of soap and asked Kara to bring him a bar. Madeline believed him. When Barry climbed naked into Kara's bed and began fondling her breasts and genitals, Kara tried to push him away, but he continued. Kara tearfully told her mother what happened, and Madeline believed her. Madeline blamed herself for not seeing the signs and believing Barry's flimsy excuses. Now, she doubts her own judgment.

Hindsight always makes it so much easier to see our mistakes. We hope no one enters a relationship expecting the other person to hurt or abuse his children. There are many things to which you can attribute a child's behavior change, moodiness, or dislike of a certain person. Just because your child stays away from your new partner doesn't mean he's abusing your child. Your child may think he tries too hard, acts too distant, wants to replace his other parent, or tells bad jokes. But, sexual abuse does happen, so be careful not to dismiss the things that are said to you or explain away unexplainable concerns.

Believing Your Child

It is easier for most parents to believe their children when the alleged perpetrator is a stranger or an acquaintance. But, what happens if your child accuses your spouse, your sibling, or your best friend? The lines get drawn no matter what you do. Someone is lying and someone is telling the truth.

Many parents want facts, answers, and reasons. Some children are old enough and mature enough to remember dates, times, and situations. Their "evidence" is irrefutable. However, a young child, or a frightened child, or a child who fears his life will fall apart with his revelation, may not seem convincing.

Obviously, everyone is innocent until proven guilty, but look at what possible reason your child could have for making a false allegation. Rarely does a child have anything to gain by lying about being abused, but a perpetrator has everything to lose by admitting guilt. Certainly, there are cases where disturbed children, usually adolescents who were abused in the past, have made false claims or been misunderstood. There are cases where some innocent remark or act gets turned into a "trumped-up charge" by a zealous or inexperienced investigator. There are cases, especially in child custody disputes, where one parent knowingly and wrongfully accuses the other parent of sexual abuse. Other times, parents misinterpret or misunderstand a child's actions or words and believe sexual abuse happened, when it didn't.

Even when sexual abuse has been proven, sometimes the wrong person gets accused. Children have been removed unfairly from their homes and families. But, despite the media coverage of horror stories, false accusations, and gross injustices, these situations are very rare. A series of checks and balances, an understanding by the child-protection team of what to look for in such cases, and the accused's right to legal counsel, usually prevents any innocent person from being found guilty. The fears parents may have about mix-ups, while real, should be weighed against the message it would give to children if measures weren't taken to try and stop the alleged perpetrator.

If someone other than your child tells you about the abuse, look at their motives, their suspicions, and their concerns. Many parents hope to prove their child is wrong because of the dreadful consequences if he's telling the truth.

> Elenor was shocked when her pre-teen daughter said her
> uncle had made lewd remarks and touched her breasts.
> Elenor wanted to believe her daughter, but she had known
> and trusted her brother all her life.

Perhaps it is easier for the family to believe such an accusation when there had been problems with the perpetrator or suspicions before the disclosure. It may be harder when the accused is a model spouse, friend, parent, etc. In these instances, the parent frequently feels a conflict about whom to trust. If you trusted someone who later turns out to be untrustworthy, it creates much doubt, anger, and a sense of betrayal.

Even if you do believe your child without hesitation, there will still be a myriad of emotions. Many parents feel they've been duped, that the offender was living a lie. Some parents are angry with themselves and feel guilty for having exposed their child to the perpetrator. Others are shocked to think that someone they loved and trusted could do this to their child and family. No matter what you think now, it is rare that every intention of the perpetrator was evil. While both you and your child understand that what the perpetrator did was wrong, it doesn't have to negate the times of genuine affection and concern.

If you suspect something is happening to your child, check out your suspicions. Talk with someone you trust about your concerns, call the child-protection worker for advice, and talk with your child. The best thing that could happen is that you're wrong. If you're right, your child will benefit from your intervention, protection, and concern. This is especially true for very young children who may not have the words to express themselves. However, because of this, there can be questions and misunderstandings.

> Damien had just been toilet trained, but he was still having problems with his bowel movements, which sometimes hurt. While his regular babysitter was on vacation, Damien's father took him to another day care. As he sat on the potty chair, Damien told the new babysitter, "Poop hurt. Daddy. Hurt me, hurt, hurt, hurt." Without knowing Damien or his family, the sitter thought the worst. In her mind, she had already tried and convicted Damien's father of sexually abusing his son.

Parents of young children need to be perceptive and look at the context in which something is said. Even verbally skilled children do not understand all the variances of language. To a three-year-old child, "someone hurting me" and "being mean to me," could run the gamut from actual abuse to appropriate discipline to nothing at all. Most parents have seen and heard their child's earth-shattering reaction to a simple request or comment and hope that no one else witnessed it because they'd suspect something terrible happened.

Young children can be difficult to understand, and often skip words in sentences or use words that sound alike. Children seek pleasure, and because a child rubs his teddy bear over the crotch of his pajamas, it doesn't mean the child's been abused. Some children are fascinated with their genitals and the "power" they have over the elimination process. "Bathroom humor," making jokes about "pooping and peeing" doesn't automatically mean abuse.

The point is that, as parents, you are the expert on your child's behavior. Take into account your child's normal reactions and the reactions common to his particular age. If you still have fears that something bad is happening to your child, then act on your concerns. However, you should be cautious about starting a witch hunt. You should have serious concerns before accusing another person of anything, especially sexual abuse. Listen to your child, ask questions, observe his behavior, follow your instincts. Use the Warning Signs lists in the first chapter as a guideline. Everyone is vulnerable —your child shouldn't be left alone with someone you suspect of hurting him, but neither should someone be accused without some evidence or legitimate concerns.

When You Don't Believe Your Child

If you have a difficult time believing your child was abused, don't just drop the subject. Find an objective outsider or professional who can help you find out what's true and decide what to do about it. It's difficult for children who are telling the truth not to be believed by their parents. On the other hand, some children lie a lot, causing their parents to wonder about everything they say. Some children, especially troubled ones, may make accusations after fights with parents, causing parents or caregivers to suspect a set-up based on revenge or anger. Some children may not tell their parents the whole story, making their parents question what they're saying.

Anita was fondled by the next-door neighbor, her father's
friend, but her father questioned her allegations. Anita told
her mother everything about the abusive incidents, but she
was embarrassed to give her father the details, so she left out
parts of the story. These omissions only confused Anita's
father, convincing him that Anita was really lying.

While children do make false accusations, it is rare. Questioning parents should look at what is interfering with their trust in their child, examine their fears and worries, and look at what it would mean to their lives if their child is telling the truth. Parents may be denying a similar personal experience and "burying their heads in the sand" about their child's abuse.

If, after all this self-examination and objective help, parents are still convinced their child is lying or was coerced to lie, help is still needed. Any child who would go to such extremes to get attention has other problems that should be addressed. If another person is behind the false accusation, that person is liable for his actions. He could be criminally prosecuted and has probably already jeopardized his relationship with the child.

Sometimes parents believe the incident happened, but the intent was not sexual. Listen to your child. Most children know the difference between a casual, accidental touch and a purposeful one. Once again, it may be the parent's wish not to believe there was a sexual connotation with the incident.

While your child was the one who was sexually abused, sexual abuse affects the whole family. Do whatever it takes to help yourself so you can be available for your child. You don't have to go through this alone. Use community resources and groups for help. You may have felt powerless to stop the abuse, but you are not powerless to begin the healing process for you and your child.

5

The Legal System

If your child is sexually abused, you'll likely become involved with the legal system. This can be frightening and confusing for you and your child. Your first involvement will be making a report to the police or a child-protection agency. That will mean an investigation and interviews with your child, and possibly with you and other witnesses. This usually happens within 72 hours after the report is made.

Each state has its mechanism for reporting and investigating sexual abuse, and no two are identical. There are even differences from county to county in any particular state. Much has been done to streamline the process and lessen the anxiety for the abused child and the family. Many counties use a community approach, where each professional involved in the case —police, child-protection worker, prosecuting attorney, and therapist— work together as a team so that each knows what the others are doing. Often, this reduces the need for numerous interviews or the child's having to repeat the story to every new person. Supposedly, all counties and states try to act in the best interests of children without interfering with the rights of the alleged perpetrators. However, it doesn't always work like this in reality, and even when it does work the way it should, the legal machinery can still be intimidating.

After the report is investigated, the prosecuting attorney decides whether there is enough evidence to prosecute the accused perpetrator. It is at this point that questions arise about such issues as who are reliable witnesses, hearsay evidence, and the reliability of the child's accusations. A case may be very clear-cut if there is medical evidence to show the abuse happened, and if the child is a good witness who can testify to dates and times and describe what happened. Most prosecuting attorneys would proceed with that kind of case. However, many cases are not so strong. Often, the child is very young and may not be a good witness, the medical exam is inconclusive, or the child can only repeat, "so and so hurt me."

To the parent of a sexually abused child, any evidence might seem to be enough, but it doesn't work that way. To prove a criminal case in court, the prosecuting attorney must have "proof beyond a reasonable doubt." However, the prosecutor will take into account admissions the child has made to others about the abuse —the child-protection team, doctor, day care provider, etc. She will look at the child's age and development to see what is appropriate or expected behavior regarding sexual knowledge and behavior. The prosecutor may seek a therapist's opinion on the child's behavior, feelings, and truthfulness about the alleged abuse and discuss the child's reaction to anatomically correct dolls. Sometimes, videotape is used in the investigation and later in court.

> Terry was only two-and-a-half years old when she said a family friend poked her "we-we" and it hurt. She couldn't remember dates or times, but only remembered it was cold outside. The child-protection worker videotaped the interview and gave Terry the anatomically correct dolls to help reenact what the perpetrator did to her. Using the dolls as models for herself and the perpetrator, Terry showed how the abuser pulled down her underwear and put his finger in her vagina. The dolls eased Terry's frustration at not knowing the "right" words to tell, and allowed her to show what happened.

Frustrations With the "System"

If the case is not accepted for prosecution, parents often feel defeated, angry, and betrayed. Certainly, if the abuser is outside of the family, you can keep her away from your child, change babysitters, or avoid the relative or friend. You may have a hard time explaining to your child why there wasn't prosecution, but do the best you can. While children should know that more evidence was needed, be careful not to blame them for the lack of evidence. It's not their fault. It may help to explain that while a court case wasn't "won," the child did win because the abuse stopped and she saw that she was believed and protected by her parents.

Accusations are not always followed by conviction and imprisonment. Even guilty people are acquitted, and sometimes they don't even go to trial. There are times when a parent without physical custody of her child, but with visitation rights or joint custody, is accused of sexual abuse and either no court case is pursued or there is an acquittal. Most custodial parents are angry that the legal system has "failed" them once, and they are fearful and worried about having their child resume unsupervised visits with the other parent. Custodial parents need to make some difficult decisions. While their options are limited, many consider further court action. However, if the matter was prosecuted once and no conviction was obtained, the accused can't be tried again for the same incident. New evidence (not previously available to the prosecution) must be presented to the court before an attorney can pursue more legal action.

Parents can teach their children new ways of self-protection, enlist the guidance of a therapist or other support person, and hope and pray nothing further happens. They can continue to keep open communication with their children, and assure them that it's okay to tell if something bad happens, despite the previous court outcome. Children need to be reassured that you believe them.

Of course, defying the law is not recommended. There are cases of national prominence where a custodial parent firmly believed her child had been sexually abused, no matter what the outcome was in court. These parents have hidden their children and spent time in jail to protect their children.

Another difficult situation is when the alleged perpetrator is a close family member, but there is not enough evidence to support legal action. It is especially stressful if other family members think you are making the whole story up. As protector of your child, you must do all you can to keep your child safe, even if it means incurring the wrath of other family members. This can be very difficult, especially if you were once close to your family. Get outside help from support groups, friends, or a therapist to keep your strength and to know that you are doing the right thing.

> Lilly believed her young son when he said Lilly's sister
> abused him. Although Lilly went to the police, there wasn't
> enough evidence to take the case to court. Lilly's family,
> including her parents, turned on her and said she made up a
> vicious lie to hurt them. They refused her calls and attempts
> to discuss what happened. Lilly knew she had done the right
> thing by standing up for her son, but now she felt she had lost
> her family.

Going to Court

If the prosecutor accepts the case, be prepared for a long process. Of course, if the accused admits guilt, a lengthy trial is avoided. Sometimes that does happen; frequently it does not.

If the case goes to trial, the question usually arises of whether the child must testify. This can be a difficult issue for parents who fear that the experience will frighten or harm their child. All abused children do not testify at the trial. The decision will depend on your child's credibility as a witness, her age, her fears, etc. This should be discussed thoroughly with the prosecuting attorney.

Following arrest, the accused will probably appear at a preliminary examination to decide whether, and how to proceed. It's not a trial, but can seem like one, because witnesses are often called and testimony is heard by a judge. If evidence at the preliminary examination establishes reason to believe the accused committed the crime charged, she will be ordered to stand trial.

Usually, the prosecuting attorney will meet with the parents and child before the preliminary hearing to discuss likely questions and explain court procedures. Sometimes, you'll visit the courtroom, and your child may be allowed to sit in the witness stand to get a feel for the situation. If you are seeing a therapist, the therapist may assist your child in preparing to testify. This is not to say that words will be put in your child's mouth. Rather, the therapist works with the prosecutor and your child so your child is as comfortable as possible talking about the abuse, is expecting certain questions, and is ready to face the alleged perpetrator in court. This can be a highly emotional time for your child, so your support is essential.

Your child may have many questions about what will happen in court. Ask her what she may be worried about or what she's afraid may happen. Some children fear looking at the perpetrator; others are worried about the questions. Some are afraid they may not remember details, and think they can't say, "I don't know," or, "I don't remember." Some worry who will be listening to the testimony. Others want to know what happens if they have to go to the bathroom or feel sick. Think about questions your child may have; look at the court experience from her perspective. Let your child know any questions are okay to ask and any fears are fine to discuss.

The Trial

Sometimes, there is no preliminary examination if the accused waives it, and the case goes directly to trial. The defense attorney and prosecuting attorney will meet with the judge for a pre-trial conference to decide whether any plea agreements can be arranged. This may include a guilty plea to a less serious offense, like assault. Many factors are involved in this decision, including the accused's record, the strength of the case, the relationship of the accused to the child, and the court's docket. Victims are often consulted by the prosecutor before a plea bargain is made, and they are entitled to be heard by the court before sentencing. If no plea is arranged, the matter is set for a specific trial date.

The time between reporting sexual abuse and the trial can be as long as a year; usually, it's between six and eight months. Hopefully, your child and possibly your family have been receiving or received some type of support or therapy. Your child will be expected to testify again at the trial. The prosecutor will again speak with you and go over questions she may ask and questions she thinks the defense attorney may ask. At this time, the defense attorney may ask to speak with you or your child about the charges, but you don't have to do it if you are uncomfortable. Any statements made by you can be used later in cross-examination by the defense attorney. Also, if you provide your statement in writing, get a copy, and never sign anything before reading it carefully. If you are approached by the defense attorney for any reason, let the prosecuting attorney know.

Sometimes, by the time your child's case reaches the trial stage, all she may want to do is forget what happened and get on with her life. However, some children are determined to see that justice is done and are eager for their day in court. Other children are fearful of the proceedings and terrified of facing the perpetrator in the court room.

If there is a jury trial in an open courtroom, your child faces the possibility of having to tell a room full of strangers about sexual acts. In our society, where so many things about healthy, appropriate, and loving sex between consenting adults is taboo, imagine how a child may feel talking about the frightening, sometimes embarrassing, possibly guilt-producing, sexual abuse. This is not meant to scare you out of court involvement. Children are more resilient than we sometimes give them credit for being, but it is meant to warn you to be sensitive to what your child may be going through.

Sometimes at this juncture, but most often before, a child may be tempted to recant or take back what she said about the abuse. This can happen when a child is unhappy with the outcome of her reporting the abuse, when she is fearful of the perpetrator, when she feels threatened, when she is afraid of the court procedures, or when she realizes the perpetrator got "into trouble" by her telling. It is not uncommon and doesn't mean your child is a liar. If your child wants to change her mind, explore her feelings about what happened and what her fears may be. Check up to see if your child (or someone your child cares about) is being threatened with bodily harm or if there are hints of harm by the perpetrator or others. Look at your own reactions and what your expectations have been. Have you been giving your child the message, either verbally or through your actions, that you wish she never told about the abuse? Don't try to solve this one alone; enlist the help of the prosecutor, therapist, or other support persons. It could be that your child was not telling the truth about the abuse, but that is very unlikely. Too often, children have the idea that once they report the abuse, everything will be fine and back to normal. They can't foresee the long court process, family disruption, or troubling emotions.

Anna was relieved when she finally told her mother that her father had been abusing her. She thought he would just stop and they could be happy again. She didn't know about her father's going to jail, her mother's constant tears, the financial burden of a lost income, or the guilt she felt for bringing this on her family. She even missed her father. To avoid further problems, Anna told her mother she had made the whole story up.

In most trials, court officials and attorneys are respectful of how frightening the trial may be for the child. In some cases, children are allowed to tell the judge and attorneys what happened in the privacy of the judge's chambers. Other times, closed circuit television is used so the child can answer questions without directly facing the accused. Small children sometimes are allowed to sit on the lap of a support person in the witness stand. Other times, the child is positioned in the stand so she is looking at the judge or support person rather than at the accused.

Many parents fear the defense attorney's questions of their child. While clearly the defense attorney will do everything possible to represent her client, she is also bound by rules and ethics. She will not be allowed to badger your child. She can question your child's motives, feelings towards the accused, circumstances surrounding the alleged abuse, memory, and truthfulness.

Sometimes, parents are subpoenaed to testify. Often, if both parent and child testify at the trial, the parent is not allowed in the courtroom during the child's testimony. For this reason, it is essential to have someone other than yourself (someone your child trusts and cares about) in the courtroom as an additional support for her. If you testify, the prosecutor should go over potential questions with you. Depending on the case, other family members, the doctor, the child-protection worker, the law enforcement officer, or the therapist may be called as witnesses. Certainly the defense may call its own witnesses, possibly even expert witnesses to dispute the prosecution's experts. Depending on the defense strategy, the alleged perpetrator may take the stand.

Reaching a Verdict

After all the testimony and closing arguments, the judge or the jury will determine guilt or innocence. Even if you did not testify at the trial, if the accused is found guilty, you can still express your views through the probation officer who writes a pre-sentence report. To do this, contact the prosecuting attorney, who will put you in touch with the probation officer. It's also appropriate at the sentencing stage for the court to suggest future restrictions on the accused's freedom, such as having no contact with the abused child or other children in the home who may also be vulnerable.

There can be mixed emotions when the perpetrator is found guilty and sentenced, especially if it is someone known to the family. There can be a sense of relief, but also some pity. Sometimes, family members are not as interested in the perpetrator's getting time in prison as in her "getting help." When there is a jail or prison sentence, some children feel guilty and believe they caused the perpetrator's problems. These children need to know the perpetrator's actions led to the jail time, not the child's telling about the abuse. Of course, in other cases, families may still be very angry and may feel the sentence was too lenient. Some families might know justice was done, but feel that no sentence can make up for what happened to their child.

While emotions can run the gamut when there is a conviction and sentence, usually one thing is predominant when a perpetrator has been found not guilty: a sense of betrayal. Commonly, families express their anger at whoever seems available, whether they see it as inept judges and attorneys, blinded juries, slick defense attorneys, or "con men" perpetrators. Their anger is real. Usually, the families feel they did everything right and still received no justice. Sometimes, however, the abused child may feel she did something wrong, whether it be crying in court or not remembering a date. While it may be difficult to give assurances when the parent is upset, the child must know that she did well. She was right to tell, and it's fine to show disappointment. Once again, it may help to realize that while the court case was lost, the child still "won" by having an end to the abuse.

Perhaps the hardest thing about acquittal for the child is the lesson that justice is not always served. She has already had the unfair situation of being sexually abused, combined with the unfair situation of the perpetrator's being set free. Unless there is irrefutable evidence, many juries are leery of convicting someone of sexual abuse. The paradox is that the juries often believe the child, but are reluctant to convict the perpetrator.

This is only a guideline to what might happen in court. There are differences in how court cases are handled in different areas. The best source of information for your family is your attorney.

6

Starting Therapy

In the previous chapters, we've suggested many times that you consult a therapist. However, some people are fearful or embarrassed about therapy because they don't know what to expect.

A therapist's job is not to judge you, but to help you through the process of healing, to answer questions, and to guide you through all the feelings you may be having. Not everyone who calls himself a therapist, whether it be a clinical social worker, psychologist, or psychiatrist is qualified to evaluate, or do ongoing therapy with sexually abused children and their families. Many highly competent professionals may not have the experience needed for successful treatment in abuse cases. Usually, you can get names of qualified therapists from the child-protection worker, attorney, or law enforcement officer working with your family. If you have doubts or questions, ask the therapist about his experience with sexually abused children. Remember, you are the consumer; a responsible therapist won't be insulted by your questions. Depending on the situation and family circumstances, you may see a therapist in private practice or one employed by a private or public agency. Some areas have a specific agency or clinic for sexually abused children. Some health insurance companies pay for therapy, others do not. Many therapists and agencies adjust or waive fees depending on your income.

Each therapist has his own style of relating to people. Some will be very direct, asking many questions right away; others may take time and let you tell them what happened at your own pace.

Despite what is a very uncomfortable subject —the abuse of your child— it is important that you and your child feel comfortable with the therapist. Certainly you may get annoyed with some of the questions, feel that things aren't going fast enough, or are going too fast, but give yourself time to get used to the idea of therapy. Feel free to ask any questions or discuss any concerns, no matter how silly, weird, or embarrassing they may seem to you.

It is not always necessary for your child to have a therapist of the same gender. It does depend on the child and circumstances. If one child who was abused by a strange man is frightened by each new man he meets, therapy could be undermined with a male therapist. For another child with similar circumstances, a caring male therapist could renew his faith that all new men won't hurt him. Certainly, the same is true for female therapists and children. A competent therapist will give you ideas or referrals as needed.

Types of Therapy

Depending on your child's age and capacity for understanding, the therapist may use play therapy as a primary treatment technique. It can be used with children of any age, but it is especially effective for children whose verbal skills are still immature and where there is little abstract thinking. Play therapy involves the use of dolls, puppets, clay, painting, drawing, story telling, free play, or any other play activity as a means to express the child's feelings. However, play therapy is not "just" playing. The therapist can help interpret your child's feelings and fears that may not or could not come out in words or may not even be in conscious thought.

> Grant, age four, was very angry with the person who abused him. He felt powerless, and began to have self-directed anger by hitting himself and banging his body against walls. During

play therapy, Grant started out using two dolls. Although he didn't identify them by name, one doll seemed to represent him; the other seemed to be the perpetrator. Initially, the "perpetrator" doll was very aggressive, but slowly the "Grant" doll began fighting back. After several months, Grant's self-abusive behavior stopped. Grant's therapy also included family therapy and he began to see his parents "take charge" by protecting him and accepting his anger.

In the above example, Grant was not able to say, "I feel powerless," but his actions pointed to that. In the case of very young children, it is important that they express themselves, but the most important thing to them may be their parents' reactions. Some parents feel that they can do "therapy" themselves at home. Without a doubt, the most therapeutic thing in the world for a sexually abused child (or any child, for that matter), is parents or caregivers who believe him, support him, and love him. However, parents or other caregivers are close to the situation and dealing with their own fears and feelings. Parents need someone objective to say what's "normal," someone to answer questions, and to say they were not to blame.

Often, parents see the therapist alone to discuss their own fears or concerns. Sometimes, parents and children visit the therapist together during play therapy sessions, and the parents learn how to help their children express their feelings and worries. Since therapy is only one part of the healing (therapy sessions generally are one or two hours per week), it is important that parents try to understand and help their children with some of the issues raised in therapy.

Although every child should have the right to confidentiality, many therapists explain before therapy begins that some things will be discussed with parents. Confidentiality may not seem important to younger children, but it is usually very important to older children and adolescents. Certainly, anything regarding someone being hurt or harmed would be discussed with parents (and possibly with a child-protection worker), but there are also many "gray areas." Therapists should explain the ground rules about confidentiality before therapy starts.

Some parents and children are relieved to hear they are not alone. While a therapist cannot, because of confidentiality, talk about specific families or circumstances, it can be comforting to know that others have been in similar situations and have come out okay.

With older children and adults, there are many specific approaches or techniques a therapist can use, but basically the therapist and client talk about his concerns. Depending on the situation, you and your therapist may decide on goals you want to see accomplished. Goals differ and depend on the person. Usually, goals pertain to the sexual abuse and your reactions, but broader topics that affect your reactions are often discussed as well. You can be working on several goals at a time. The following are some goals common in therapy of this nature:

• Discuss details of the abuse.
• Find appropriate outlets for anger.
• End nightmares.
• Lessen depression and sadness.
• Get through the court process.
• Begin to trust others.
• Explore feelings of guilt and shame.
• Put responsibility for the abuse on the perpetrator, not self.
• Begin to appreciate personal strengths and talents.

There can be as many goals as there are sexually abused children and their families. Things are not accomplished overnight. For some people, it is a struggle to even trust the therapist, making it difficult to accomplish any other goals until trust is established.

Other forms of therapy are family therapy and group therapy. Many families want the opportunity to talk together and communicate their feelings. Sometimes, families need to "clear the air," and let one another know how the abuse has affected them. Some children and their families benefit from group therapy — therapy with others who have had similar experiences. Some children need to know that they were not singled out. (Often their compassion for one another is remarkable.)

> Seven girls, ages six to ten, were in a group for sexually abused children. Hannah struggled with the guilt after she was abused, feeling that she could have done something to stop it. After hearing the group members' stories about their abuse and giving them advice, Hannah began to understand for herself what she had been telling the other group members: it was not her fault.

One form of therapy is not necessarily better than the other. All are different ways of trying to achieve the same thing. Many children are involved at one time or another in all types: play therapy, family therapy, and group therapy. Group therapy has proven invaluable for many children; there is something to be said for strength in numbers regarding healing.

Therapy Issues

Many therapy issues arise with sexually abused children.[4] Here are some common ones:
- Trust: When a child is abused, his trust of adults is undermined (particularly if the perpetrator was an adult family member). Psychological damage to the child depends, in part, on how long the abuse went on, how frequent it was, who the perpetrator was, and the reaction of family members. It is important for the child to have different relationships with people who are trustworthy.

- Feeling Unclean or Dirty: Children often think there is something wrong with them. Some adults and children perpetuate this myth by avoiding a child who has been sexually abused, or by thinking he is bad or sexually promiscuous.
- Guilt Feelings and Feeling Responsible: Children can feel responsible for destroying the family, e.g., when an abusive father moves out, a child is placed in foster care, or a mother has more financial burdens. Many children feel guilty if they enjoyed the attention, nurturance, or touch, but not the sexual abuse. (In some cases, the only time the perpetrator is attentive to the child is during the abuse.)
- Anger: Children need to focus on their angry feelings toward the perpetrator, family, or the "system." Sometimes, a child will react inappropriately with anger by being aggressive, incorrigible, or truant. Sometimes, children will put themselves in a position to be punished or do things that are self-destructive.
- Understanding the Meaning of Sexual Abuse: Children need to understand the dynamics of sexual abuse. This includes knowing that the abuse was not their fault and that the perpetrator was responsible.
- Self-Protection: Children need to learn how to protect themselves and not be vulnerable "next time."
- Self-Esteem: There should be a focus on the child's strengths and talents, so the child identifies himself as something other than a "sexual abuse victim."

Along with the above issues, the therapist will most likely touch on these themes with sexually abused children:
- Believing them.
- Praising their courage for telling what happened.
- Acknowledging that what the perpetrator did was wrong.
- Letting them know the abuse was not their fault.
- Listening to their fears and feelings.
- Asking them what they want.
- Letting them know any feelings are "okay."

- Being truthful with them.
- Allowing them to tell things at their own pace.
- Committing to work together on healing.

Therapy can help even in families where one parent was the perpetrator. However, the treatment in such cases will take a long time, and the entire family must make a commitment to therapy and making changes. The other parent must still provide the belief, trust, and support for the child, while deciding whether the marriage is worth trying to save. While sexual abuse in the family doesn't automatically mean divorce, frequently it does.

In addition to ongoing therapy, your child or family may be asked to have an evaluation. Frequently, this is requested by the child-protection worker to get the therapist's opinion about the child and the validity of the allegation, to gather more information, or to help the child and family through the crisis. The evaluation may be what leads to ongoing therapy.

Healing

Healing after sexual abuse is a process, and will probably go on long after therapy has stopped. If your child is old enough, he may always remember what happened to him, but you hope he can put it in perspective and not let it affect his whole life. Therapy cannot and may not "fix everything." Everyone needs to make his own decisions about his life. However, therapy can offer some guidance, hope, and an outlet for some feelings. The therapist cannot make it so the abuse never happened, cannot work miracles, and cannot give you all the answers. In order for therapy to work, the child and family must be willing to work hard and be committed to making things better. Therapy is not done "to" you; you are the key. Of course, there are times when no matter how committed the family or how experienced the therapist, things just don't seem right. In those circumstances, talk to your therapist about your concerns, you may both decide changing therapists is an option.

However, constantly changing therapists is not an answer. You may get angry or upset with your therapist at times, but this doesn't necessarily mean you have to switch therapists; it may mean you don't want to find out the answers and the therapist is getting "too close." Therapists can help fit the "pieces" to the puzzle of your feelings, worries, or uncertainties. Some people may not know why they are reacting a certain way until some questions are answered and some feelings are unraveled. Some people may have consciously forgotten circumstances in their lives that directly affect how they deal with their own or their child's abuse.

There is no set length of time therapy should go on. It could be a one-time evaluation or years of therapy, depending on the person and the circumstances. An average would be three to nine months. However, many people benefit from additional therapy at different stages in their lives. New concerns may arise when the child begins puberty, becomes sexually active, marries, or has children of his own.[5] Some people may choose to stay in therapy to deal with other problems after some peace has been made about the sexual abuse.

While there are no guarantees, the benefits of therapy outweigh any desire to hide or never discuss the abuse. The outcome of silence has been generations of children who grew up believing they were at fault.

Although consulting a competent therapist is recommended, don't overlook other sources of support and strength. Talking with a friend, family member, support group, clergyman, or spiritual adviser could be invaluable. Do whatever it takes to help your child and your family.

7

Ideas for Prevention

Although your child may already have been sexually abused, you probably have concerns about preventing further abuse and protecting any other children in the family. While there may always be child sexual abuse, there are many ways of avoiding potential danger. The keys are preparation, empowerment, and education. Your child needs to know what to do, when to do it, what to avoid, and believe she has the right to be assertive about protecting herself.

> A man stopped his car at the corner on Maggie's way home
> from school. He said her baby brother was sick and her
> mother wanted him to bring Maggie to the hospital. Maggie
> had never seen the man before and knew she shouldn't go
> with strangers. Maggie shouted, "No, you're lying!" and ran
> to a girlfriend's house, where they called Maggie's mother
> and the police.

Children need to know they have the right to stand up for themselves, to question something an adult or child may ask them to do that doesn't seem right, and to have control over their own bodies. They should know that sexual abuse can happen to anyone, and that the perpetrator can be a stranger, friend, or relative. They need to know that adults don't ask children to do "adult things," and that if someone asks them to do something wrong or uncomfortable, they should tell a parent or other trusted adult.

Perhaps one of the most important lessons any child can get from her parents is a healthy respect for herself, her body, and other people. These lessons begin early in life, not just when a child is ready for school. Even in infancy, children can get the parents' message that they respect their needs and desires.

> At a family gathering, five-month-old Lee couldn't tolerate the constant juggling and holding between relatives, and he began to cry. His father quickly took him to a quiet spot and held him. For the rest of the afternoon, Lee enjoyed watching his new relatives from the comfort of his father's arms.

Children learn from example. If parents think their child and her feelings are important, then the child can learn she has the right to say "no" to protect herself; she learns to keep no secrets from her parents; and she knows someone will listen to her if she talks about her fears.

Informing Your Child

Besides feelings of self-worth, every child needs some specific information about avoiding sexual abuse. As your child grows, she should have more information. Toddlers and pre-schoolers may ask about birth and where babies come from. They will start toilet training and have questions about their bodies; many children are fascinated with their genitals at this age. They need correct, but simple information. Children should learn the proper names for their genitals, but many families have their own private names, too. Whatever you call these areas, it should be taught as matter-of-factly as you teach the name of an elbow or an ear, without shame or embarrassment. The difference is that children should learn that these body parts are private, but not because they're dirty or bad. Sometimes, it helps to talk about the "bathing-suit" parts of the body, so children know what should be private and covered.

Parents of very young children should begin to talk about safety issues, appropriate touching, and the differences between "good touch" and "bad touch." Respect and privacy should be taught and given to all family members. Parents should emphasize that there should be no secrets in the family. Children should know "I'm going to tell" is a powerful deterrent to abuse.

As your child gets older, there are more opportunities for her to be away from home. Children need to know about love and relationships, and to have correct information about sex, sexuality, "date rape," masturbation, menstruation, nocturnal emissions, AIDS and other sexually transmitted diseases. This is the time to dispel any myths your child may have about these issues or any other personal subjects. Children should be wary of strangers, suspicious of odd requests, and refuse to keep secrets about someone being harmed, about something illegal, or about anything they question as wrong. They should be taught to respect authority, but not to trust blindly anyone who wears a uniform or looks official. They need to be taught to tell their parents, caregivers, or other trusted adults about any concerns, unwanted advances, or something that makes them scared or uneasy.

Teaching Safety

Often, parents teach prevention and safety without realizing it. Many of the following guidelines for preventing sexual abuse or other types of harm are common sense:
- Establish family rules for what to do in an emergency.
- Let your child know who would take care of her in an emergency.
- Teach your child her phone number and address.

- Know your child's whereabouts.
- Let your child know your whereabouts and how you can be reached.
- Know your child's friends, associates, and employers.
- Check references and get background information on people to whom you entrust your child: babysitters, youth-group leaders, coaches, etc.
- Never leave a young child alone at home; tell older children not to open the door to anyone.
- Never leave your child with someone you don't know or trust.
- Don't leave young children alone in a car or in any public place.
- Have a "buddy system" so your child is with someone else while walking home from school, going to the store, etc.
- Teach your child how to handle phone calls: never say she's alone, and hang up immediately if the call is obscene or scary.
- Teach your child emergency phone numbers and keep them by the phone.
- Teach your child to avoid strangers, deserted areas, or places with few exits, such as alleys or stairways.
- Teach your child to walk near the curb, facing traffic.
- Tell your child that if a car approaches to walk away in a direction opposite to the car, and to go somewhere safe.
- Establish a neighborhood system of "safe houses" (of people you know and trust) where children can go if scared or approached by someone.
- Emphasize that your child and her safety are more important than property.
- Teach your child that you'd rather have her "overreact" and be embarrassed, than "underreact" and get hurt.
- Teach your child to listen to her own feelings and judgments about a person or situation, especially when she's frightened or uneasy.
- Avoid having your child's name, age, address, or picture together where anyone could see it, such as a newspaper, community directory, or on clothing.

Many parents wonder how to approach these lessons with their children. Most parents have no problem teaching safety rules about such things as not touching hot stoves or running into streets. The method is the same for the safety rules about preventing sexual abuse. You present it in a calm manner, at appropriate times, keep reminding your child periodically, and be consistent with the message. Some parents find a "what-if" game helpful.

> Sandy and her parents were playing in the park. A man approached them to ask for directions. Sandy's parents took the opportunity to ask her what she would have done if she were alone or with her girlfriend and the same thing happened.

The "what-if" game can be personalized for your child. Don't make it an interrogation; use it as a fun learning tool. Use your knowledge of your child and her likes and dislikes. Your child may know not to talk to strangers, but what if that stranger offers her a ride on a motorcycle, and your child is enthralled by anything that goes fast and makes loud noises? Take the opportunity when new situations arise in your child's life to ask her questions in a non-threatening way. Get reactions to new babysitters, teachers, group leaders, etc. Be aware if your child has a "crush" on a friend's older brother or the neighbor next door, or if someone seems unusually interested in her.

You should respond to your child's answers with praise for appropriate responses or give other options or ideas if her answers were wrong or only half-right. Some children answer with bravado (e.g., "I'd put him in prison," or, "I'd karate chop him.") You should make sure your child gives realistic responses and if not, be her reality check.

> When you're big like Mommy or Daddy maybe you could
> karate chop him and get away, but you're six and a lot
> smaller than an adult... Let's think of something a six-year-
> old could do.

Another way of giving your child some direction and answers is through storytelling. You can either make up stories or use real examples about a child dealing correctly with a difficult situation. After the story, you can ask your child how she would have handled the problem. Discuss your child's answer, elaborate on it, and give other appropriate answers if necessary.

Children need to know boundaries and understand their right to have personal space. As always, parents should respect their child's needs. Children can be taught to set their own limits. Talk with them about the times they feel uncomfortable. It could include the times someone stares at them, tickles them too much, pinches their cheeks, or stands too close to them. Help them identify those uncomfortable feelings and how their body responds. Discuss ways to handle the situation. Realize that your child will probably feel more intimidated when the violator is an adult, rather than a child. Discuss the differences.

> Benny ran home from the neighborhood store. He told his
> mother some "weird looking guy" kept staring at him, and
> left the store right after he did, following Benny to the corner.
> Benny admitted he was scared. His face was hot and his heart
> was pounding, and he didn't calm down until he was safely
> home.

Saying No

As discussed earlier, saying "NO" is a powerful tool. Practice saying no with your child about different situations. Find out from your child why she might not say no (e.g., to avoid hurting someone's feelings or seeming rude). Think about other possible reasons. Once again, note the differences between a child's saying no to another child and saying no to an adult. Reinforce with your child that it's okay to say no to anyone if they're scared, uncertain about what's being asked, or merely feel "funny" about a situation. Although no parent wants her child to lie, let your child know it's okay to stretch the truth in order to protect herself or feel safe.

While talking with your child and preparing her to be wary about sexual abuse is no guarantee that it won't happen, it will give her the tools and confidence to know what to do if approached. Prevention techniques work far better than scare tactics. Every child needs to have accurate, useful information, and not to feel constantly scared and unsure of herself. To avoid talking about the dangers of sexual abuse or merely scaring a child about life's dangers is a disservice to the child. All of us do better when we're prepared for a situation.

Relieving Parents' Fears

Some parents fear that a child who has been abused may grow up to abuse others. They want to prevent any future problems with their child or someone else's child.

There are many theories why some people sexually abuse children, but there is no clear cut answer; the reasons are complex. Although many perpetrators were abused as children, this does not mean your child will grow up to abuse others. Sexual abuse is more about power and control than about sex.

There are circumstances other than sexual abuse as a child that lead adults to become sexually abusive to children. Most perpetrators share the feeling of worthlessness. Many are lonely and seek a child's unconditional acceptance. Some act from rage or as a reaction to their own histories of violence, abuse, or neglect. Some perpetrators rationalize that they are a "friend" to lonely or isolated children and give them the affection their busy or overwhelmed parents do not. Many had distant or uncaring families and little emotional support while growing up. All have a skewed sense of boundaries and limits regarding appropriate behavior. Some lead "perfectly normal" lives until a serious stress or setback triggers their abusive behavior. Some perpetrators blame their behavior and lack of inhibition on alcohol or drugs.

It's a safe bet that an abused child who receives love, support, and understanding after sexual abuse will show these same qualities when she's older. Children who have compassion and a sense of self-worth, and who know appropriate limits, do not grow up to be sexual offenders.

Once again, the ideas presented in this chapter are guidelines. Many school districts teach child safety lessons, often in cooperation with local law enforcement agencies. Some schools may teach more controversial subjects such as sex education. It's a good idea to know what the school programs are teaching. It will help you reinforce the idea of prevention at home and avoid confusing your child with any conflicting messages. If you disagree with what is being taught at school, you'll have to decide what to do. Some parents disagree publicly and may take action; others address the mixed signals in the privacy of their home with their children. The most important thing is that your child learns how to protect herself against abuse.

Appendix A
Definitions of Child Sexual Abuse

CHILD SEXUAL ABUSE is tricking, manipulating, threatening, or forcing a child into sexual contact with an adult (and sometimes, an older child). Sexual abuse involves physical contact such as fondling, oral sex, or penetration of the anus or vagina. It also includes non-physical offenses, such as sexual comments, obscene phone calls, indecent exposure, or voyeurism.

An adult who abuses a child uses his power and dominance to coerce the child into sexual compliance. The child can be either threatened outright or led to believe he should do what the abuser wants. Perpetrators can play all types of "mind games" with children, using force, threats, sympathy, friendship, or fear.

Incest is commonly thought of as any sexual activity between family members. This would include blood relationships, such as a parent and child, siblings, and grandparent and child, as well as stepparent-stepchild relationships. The impact of sexual abuse on a child is the same whether it's a blood relative or not. More important to the child would be the family relationship and kinship roles between the perpetrator and child, rather than the presence or absence of blood ties. It would be equally traumatic for a child whether the perpetrator was a birth parent or a stepparent who raised him.

The following list outlines some sexually abusive behavior[6]:

- Nudity, disrobing, or exposing the genitals, for the purpose of arousing the adult or the child.
- Watching a child undress, urinate, or bathe, for the purpose of arousing the adult or the child.
- Kissing a child in a lingering or unusually intimate way.
- Masturbation, oral sex, or other sexual fondling between the adult and the child.

- Sexual penetration of the child by the adult or the adult by the child. This can involve penetration of any body opening, including the vagina, mouth, or anus, and can involve penetration by a penis, fingers, or other objects (abusers have been known to use everything from crayons to bottles).
- Forcing or encouraging a child to engage in sexual activity with another child or adult.
- Exposing a child to sexual activity or exhibitionism for the purpose of arousing or gratifying another.
- Allowing a child to engage in sexual activity inappropriate for the child's age.
- Using a child in photographs or films or other performances of a sexual nature, regardless of whether the material is legally "obscene."

Appendix B
Laws Pertaining to Child Sexual Abuse

EACH STATE HAS LAWS protecting the rights of children and making it illegal to physically, emotionally, or sexually abuse or exploit a child. These laws are very specific and involve pages of detailed examples. For instance, Michigan's Child Protection Law[7] clearly defines child abuse, neglect, sexual abuse, and sexual exploitation. It outlines who must report suspicions of abuse and provides for the protection of children, legal counsel, and the authorization of medical exams.

The Criminal Sexual Conduct Statute of Michigan[8] defines sexual abuse as a crime. It covers four "degrees" of sexual misconduct. While the entire law fills pages, the following list summarizes each of the degrees of abuse.

- First Degree Criminal Sexual Conduct (CSC): Sexual penetration with someone under the age of thirteen or with someone between the ages of thirteen and sixteen if force or coercion is used, if both are related or members of the same household, if the perpetrator is in a position of authority, or if the perpetrator has reason to know the victim is mentally or physically incapacitated.

- Second Degree CSC: Sexual contact with someone under the age of thirteen or with someone between the ages of thirteen and sixteen if force or coercion is used, if both are related or members of the same household, if the perpetrator is in a position of authority, or if the perpetrator has reason to know the victim is mentally or physically incapacitated.

- Third Degree CSC: Sexual penetration with someone between the ages of thirteen and sixteen or if force or coercion is used, or if the perpetrator has reason to know the victim is mentally or physically incapacitated.

• Fourth Degree CSC: Sexual contact with force or coercion or if the perpetrator has reason to know the victim is mentally or physically incapacitated.

Coercion is defined by law as force, threat, or fear of violence. Sexual penetration includes sexual intercourse, cunnilingus, fellatio, or any intrusion, however slight, into a person's body. This could involve either the genital or anal openings, with or without the presence of semen.

Sexual contact is the intentional touching of a victim's or perpetrator's intimate parts or the touching of clothing covering those intimate parts. To be abuse, the touching must be reasonably construed as being for the purpose of sexual arousal, not unintentional nor accidental.

Lastly, the current trend in legislation is to protect victims after a crime has been committed. While such laws cannot begin to compensate people for crimes against them, they do address the need for their input. Michigan's Crime Victims' Rights Act,[9] for instance, provides that the victim be notified if the defendant is released before trial, that the victim can confer with the prosecutor about jury selection, and that, whenever possible, there be a separate waiting area outside a courtroom for the victim and defendant. It allows the victim to have input during the court process and to be notified of the court's disposition of the case, the defendant's release dates, and escapes. This law also has provisions for some financial restitution and the protection of privacy.

---

*All the examples are from the State of Michigan. However, most states have similar laws.

Bibliography
Additional Resources for Parents and Children

MANY BOOKS, materials, and services are available for children and parents regarding sexual abuse, prevention, and safety issues. The following lists have some book suggestions. Your librarian, bookseller, therapist, or support person may give you other ideas. Also, most of the listed books have their own suggestions for recommended reading.

For Young Children

These books should be read with your child, so any questions can be answered. All of the books are appropriate for young children, but where possible, a suggested age is given.[10] However, your child's maturity and level of understanding may be a more accurate guide for choosing a book than his reading level or age.

Bassett, Kerry. *My Very Own Special Body Book.* Redding, California: Hawthorne Press, 1987. (pre-school to grade 2)

Buschman, Janis, and Debbie Hunley. *Strangers Don't Look Like the Big Bad Wolf.* Edmonds, Washington: The Chas. Franklin Press,1985. (grades 2 to 4)

Dayee, Frances. *Private Zone.* Edmonds, Washington: The Chas. Franklin Press,1982.

Freeman, Lory. *It's My Body.* Seattle, Washington: Parenting Press, Inc., 1983. (pre-school to grade 3)

Girard, Linda Walvoord. *My Body Is Private.* Niles, Illinois: Albert Whitman and Company, 1992. (grades 1 to 5)

Girard, Linda Walvoord. *Who Is a Stranger and What Should I Do?* Niles, Illinois: Albert Whitman and Company, 1985. (grades 2 to 6)

Johnsen, Karen. *The Trouble With Secrets.* Seattle, Washington: Parenting Press, Inc., 1986. (pre-school to grade 3)

Kehoe, Patricia. *Something Happened and I'm Scared to Tell: A Book for Young Children Victims of Abuse.* Seattle, Washington: Parenting Press, Inc., 1987. (pre-school to grade 1)

Krause, Elaine. *Speak Up, Say No!* Oregon City, Oregon: Krause House, 1989. (pre-school to grade 3)

Meyer, Linda. *Safety Zone: A Book Teaching Child Abduction Prevention Skills.* Edmonds, Washington: The Chas. Franklin Press, 1984. (kindergarten to grade 6)

Spencer, Steven, and Laurie A. White. *Take Care With Yourself: A Young Person's Guide to Understanding, Preventing, and Healing from the Hurts of Child Abuse.* Harbor Springs, Michigan: White and Spencer, 1983. (kindergarten to grade 7)

Wachter, Oralee. *No More Secrets for Me.* Boston: Little, Brown and Company, 1984. (grades 1 to 4)

For Older Children and Adolescents

While you probably won't be reading these books to your child, it's a good idea to read them yourself so you'll be able to discuss them with your child. Be available for questions, comments, or to clear up any misconceptions or confusing ideas.

Benedict, Helen. *Safe, Strong, & Streetwise: The Teenager's Guide to Preventing Sexual Assault.* Boston: Little, Brown and Company, 1987. (grades 7 and up)

Cooney, Judith. *Coping With Sexual Abuse.* New York: Rosen Publishing Group, Inc., 1991. (grades 7 to 12)

Fay, Jennifer, and Billie J. Flerchinger. *Top Secret: Sexual Assault Information for Teenagers Only.* Renton, Washington: King County

Rape Relief, 1982.

Hyde, Margaret. *Sexual Abuse: Let's Talk About It.* Philadelphia: The Westminster Press, 1987. (grades 5 and up)

Stark, Evan. *Everything You Need to Know About Sexual Abuse.* New York: Rosen Publishing Group, Inc., 1990. (grades 7 to 12)

Terkel, Susan, and Janice E. Rench. *Feeling Safe, Feeling Strong: How to Avoid Sexual Abuse and What to Do if It Happens to You.* Minneapolis: Lerner Publications Company, 1984. (grades 4 to 8)

For Parents and Other Caregivers

Adams, Caren, and Jennifer Fay. *No More Secrets: Protecting Your Child from Sexual Assault.* San Luis Obispo, California: Impact Publishers, 1981.

Adams, Caren, Jennifer Fay, and Jan Loreen-Martin. *NO Is Not Enough: Helping Teenagers Avoid Sexual Assault.* San Luis Obispo, California: Impact Publishers, 1984.

Hagans, Kathryn, and Joyce Case. *When Your Child Has Been Molested: A Parent's Guide to Healing and Recovery.* New York: Lexington Books, 1988.

Hart-Rossi, Janie. *Protect Your Child from Sexual Abuse: A Parent's Guide.* Seattle, Washington: Parenting Press, Inc., 1984.

For Parents and Caregivers Who Were Abused As Children

Bass, Ellen, and Laura Davis. *The Courage to Heal.* New York: Harper and Row, 1988.

Bass, Ellen, and Louise Thorton, eds. *I Never Told Anyone: Writings by Women Survivors of Child Sexual Abuse.* New York: Harper and Row, 1983.

Blume, E. Sue. *Secret Survivors: Uncovering Incest and Its Aftereffects in Women.* New York: Ballantine Books, 1991.

Callaghan, Linda. *Inrage: Healing the Hidden Rage of Child Sexual Abuse.* Traverse City, Michigan: Neahtawanta Press, 1991.

Davis, Laura. *The Courage to Heal Workbook.* New York: Harper and Row, 1990.

Forward, Susan, and Craig Buck. *Betrayal of Innocence: Incest and Its Devastation.* New York: Penguin Books, 1988.

Grubman-Black, Stephen. *Broken Boys / Mending Men.* New York: Ivy Books, 1990.

Hunter, Mic. *Abused Boys: The Neglected Victims of Sexual Abuse.* New York: Fawcett Columbine, 1990.

Lew, Mike. *Victims No Longer: Men Recovering from Incest and Other Sexual Child Abuse.* New York: Harper Collins Publishers, 1990.

Petersen, Betsy. *Dancing With Daddy: A Childhood Lost and a Life Regained.* New York: Bantam Books, 1991.

Poston, Carol, and Karen Lison. *Reclaiming Our Lives: Hope for Adult Survivors of Incest.* Boston: Little, Brown and Company, 1989.

Notes

[1] National Center on Child Abuse and Neglect. *National Child Abuse and Neglect Data System: Working Paper 2- 1991 Summary Data Component.* Washington, DC: U.S. Government Printing Office, 1993.

[2] National Center on Child Abuse and Neglect. *National Child Abuse and Neglect Data System: Working Paper 2 - 1991 Summary Data Component.* 1993. (See entry #1)

[3] Adapted from Educational and Training Materials from Child and Family Services, Traverse City, Michigan and the National Center on Child Abuse and Neglect, Washington, D.C.

[4] Adapted from *Treatment of the Victim* by Kathleen Coulborn Faller, Ph.D. ACSW from the 1986 manual of the Community Approach to Child Sexual Abuse, Interdisciplinary Project on Child Abuse and Neglect, The University of Michigan, Ann Arbor, Michigan.

[5] Faller, Kathleen Coulborn. *Treatment of the Victim.* Ann Arbor: The University of Michigan Interdisciplinary Project on Child Abuse and Neglect, 1986. (See entry # 4)

[6] Adapted from Educational and Training Materials from Child and Family Services and the National Center on Child Abuse and Neglect. (See entry # 3)

[7] Child Protection Law: MCL § 722.621; MSA § 25.248 et seq.

[8] Criminal Sexual Conduct Law: MCL § 750.520; MSA § 28.788 et seq.

[9] Crime Victims' Rights Act: MCL § 780.751; MSA § 28.1287 et seq.

[10] *Children's Books in Print: 1993 Volume 2.* New Providence, New Jersey: R.R.Bowker, 1993.

References

Adams, Caren, and Jennifer Fay. *No More Secrets: Protecting Your Child from Sexual Assault*. San Luis Obispo, California: Impact Publishers, 1981.

Bass, Ellen, and Laura Davis. *The Courage to Heal*. New York: Harper and Row, 1988.

Faller, Kathleen Coulborn. *Treatment of the Victim*. Ann Arbor, Michigan: The University of Michigan Interdisciplinary Project on Child Abuse and Neglect (training manual), 1986.

National Center on Child Abuse and Neglect. *National Child Abuse and Neglect Data System: Working Paper 2 - 1991 Summary Data Component*. Washington, DC: US Government Printing Office, 1993.

Poston, Carol, and Karen Lison. *Reclaiming Our Lives: Hope for Adult Survivors of Incest*. Boston: Little, Brown and Company, 1989.

– – – –. *Sexual Abuse: Causes, Consequences, and Treatment of Incestuous and Pedophilic Acts*. Holmes Beach, Florida: Learning Publications, Inc., 1985.

Taylor, Marilyn, and Cliva Mee. *What Abused and Neglected Children Need*. Kansas City, Missouri: The Children's Place.

Veresh, Carolyn. *Guiding the Sexual Development of Your Foster Child*. Ypsilanti, Michigan: Eastern Michigan University, 1978.

Whitcomb, Debra. "Prosecuting Child Sexual Abuse - New Approaches." National Institute of Justice, NIJ Reports/SNI 197, May 1986, 2-6.

Resources

Child and Family Services
Traverse City, Michigan 49685

Gratiot County Child Advocacy Association
Alma, Michigan 48801

Interdisciplinary Project on Child Abuse and Neglect
The University of Michigan
Social Work Center Building
1015 East Huron
Ann Arbor, Michigan 48104

Michigan Department of Social Services
Kalkaska County
Kalkaska, Michigan 49646

National Center on Child Abuse and Neglect
330 C Street SW
Washington, D.C. 20201

National Clearinghouse on Child Abuse and Neglect
P.O. Box 1182
Washington, D.C. 20013

* These were resources used by the author during the book's development.

Index

SELF HELP / CHILD ABUSE

The Sexually Abused Child: A Parent's Guide to Coping & Understanding—

- **Uses case examples and practical suggestions**
- **Discusses both the child's and the parent's feelings and reactions**
- **Gives a step-by-step account of the legal process**
- **Focuses on hope and help through prevention ideas and therapy**

CHILDREN ARE SEXUALLY ABUSED every day. It is a shocking and frightening part of our society. It is also a parent's nightmare. Few caregivers are prepared to deal with the reality and handle the consequences of their child's sexual abuse.

In this warm and reassuring book, *Kathleen Flynn Mach* gives parents the information they need to help themselves and their child. **The Sexually Abused Child: A Parent's Guide to Coping & Understanding** relieves fears, offers hope, and helps families cope and thrive after the trauma of sexual abuse.

66 This book provides an invaluable tool to offer families when child sexual abuse has occurred. It is clearly written, practical, and will help those families on the road to recovery." *–Douglas J. Newman, M.D., Duluth Clinic*

66 A very informative book on a very sensitive subject. A must read for parents, school personnel, and everyone who cares about kids." *–Mary L. Schols, M.S.W., Illinois Public Schools*

66 I really enjoyed the clear, common sense, down-to-earth writing. I especially felt the variety of reactions in the child cases and the details of the trial were helpful. I've never seen this sort of help before." *–Evelyn Petersen, M.A., Education/Parenting Consultant & Columnist for the Detroit Free Press*

Kathleen Flynn Mach, MSW is a clinical social worker who has counseled abused children and their families since 1980. She is a member of the Academy of Certified Social Workers *and a* Board Certified Diplomate in Clinical Social Work. *Currently, she is in private practice in northern Michigan.*

Family Insight Books
WILLIAMSBURG, MICHIGAN

Cover design by Heather Lee Shaw

$9.95 U.S.A.
$13.00 Canada

ISBN 0-9640778-0-9

50995

9 780964 077805